TRANSACTIONS

OF THE

AMERICAN PHILOSOPHICAL SOCIETY

HELD AT PHILADELPHIA
FOR PROMOTING USEFUL KNOWLEDGE

NEW SERIES—VOLUME 64, PART 8
1974

THE IMPERIAL LIBRARY IN SOUTHERN SUNG CHINA, 1127–1279

A Study of the Organization and Operation of the Scholarly Agencies
of the Central Government

JOHN H. WINKELMAN

State University College of Arts and Science, Geneseo, New York

THE AMERICAN PHILOSOPHICAL SOCIETY

INDEPENDENCE SQUARE

PHILADELPHIA

December, 1974

PUBLICATIONS

OF

The American Philosophical Society

The publications of the American Philosophical Society consist of PROCEEDINGS, TRANSACTIONS, MEMOIRS, and YEAR BOOK.

THE PROCEEDINGS contains papers which have been read before the Society in addition to other papers which have been accepted for publication by the Committee on Publications. In accordance with the present policy one volume is issued each year, consisting of six bimonthly numbers, and the price is $5.00 net per volume.

THE TRANSACTIONS, the oldest scholarly journal in America, was stated in 1769 and is quarto size. In accordance with the present policy each annual volume is a collection of monographs, each issued as a part. The current annual subscription price is $15,00 net per volume. Individual copies of the TRANSACTIONS are offered for sale. This issue is priced at $5.00.

Each volume of the MEMOIRS is published as a book. The titles cover the various fields of learning; most of the recent volumes have been historical. The price of each volume is determind by its size and character.

The YEAR BOOK is of considerable interest to scholars because of the reports on grants for research and to libraries for this reason and because of the section dealing with the acquisitions of the Library. In addition it contains the Charter and Laws, and lists of present and former members, and reports of committees and meetings. The YEAR BOOK is published about April 1 for the preceding calendar year. The current price is $5.00.

An author desiring to submit a manuscript for publication should send it to the Editor, George W. Corner, American Philosophical Society, 104 South Fifth Street, Philadelphia, Pa. 19106.

TRANSACTIONS

OF THE

AMERICAN PHILOSOPHICAL SOCIETY

HELD AT PHILADELPHIA
FOR PROMOTING USEFUL KNOWLEDGE

NEW SERIES—VOLUME 64, PART 8
1974

THE IMPERIAL LIBRARY IN SOUTHERN SUNG CHINA, 1127–1279

A Study of the Organization and Operation of the Scholarly Agencies
of the Central Government

JOHN H. WINKELMAN

State University College of Arts and Science, Geneseo, New York

THE AMERICAN PHILOSOPHICAL SOCIETY
INDEPENDENCE SQUARE
PHILADELPHIA

December, 1974

To

OTIS D. RICHARDSON

Teacher

Publication of the two large architectural draw-
ings accompanying the book was made possible
by a grant to the author from the American
Council of Learned Societies.

PREFACE

One of the most distinctive characteristics of Chinese society is its tradition of scholarship. Yet to date it has not been clearly delineated as an area of study as have government, economics, science, poetry, and art. The social setting in which the scholar worked and the tradition of which he was a part remain largely unknown; yet we know that it conditioned his results.

This study is an attempt to shed light on an aspect of the tradition of scholarship in Southern Sung China (1127–1279), namely the organization and operation of the principal scholarly agencies of the central government. These agencies were the chief means by which the government fulfilled its obligation to foster the pursuit of scholarship in society as well as to serve its own administrative needs.

The author is fortunate to have had the financial assistance of the American Philosophical Society and the scholarly advice of Professor Edward A. Kracke, Jr.; however, neither one bears the responsibility for errors of fact or judgment in the text. These are borne by the author alone.   J.H.W.

THE IMPERIAL LIBRARY IN SOUTHERN SUNG CHINA, 1127–1279
A Study of the Organization and Operation of the Scholarly Agencies of the Central Government

JOHN H. WINKELMAN

CONTENTS

PAGE

I. Government and the pursuit of scholarship
The pursuit of scholarship 5
The canon of orthodox belief 6
Document compilation and historiography ....
Libraries and archives 7
II. Buildings and grounds
Capital city of Hang-chou 12
Imperial Library building complex 15
Imperial Library area 15
Compilation and history area 17
Rest and contemplation area 18
Service area 18
III. Administration and personnel
Administrative hierarchy of government 18
Imperial Library directive personnel positions and
quotas 19
Imperial Library directive personnel quotas and
appointments, 1131–1190 21
Imperial Library directive personnel as an elite group
within the civil service 22
Tenure of office and continuity of policy implemen-
tation 23
Operative personnel 24
Service personnel 26
IV. Scholarship and books
Document compilation and history writing 26
Reconstitution of the Imperial Library collections .. 27
Processing of works for the collections 32
Characteristics of the collections 33
Use of the collections 37
Appendix
I. The Imperial Library building complex 40
II. Imperial Library wage schedules and personnel data 41
III. List of Chinese characters 46
Bibliography 53
Index 61

I. GOVERNMENT AND THE PURSUIT OF SCHOLARSHIP

Under the Sung dynasty (960–1279) the long and distinguished Chinese scholarly tradition entered its age of maturity. Great writers of essays and other forms of literary prose emerged. Poetry, which had enjoyed a golden age beginning in the eighth century, evolved new forms and proliferated in original and subtle expressions. The old craft of history-writing was supplemented by new models thereby producing a body of historical writing perhaps unrivaled as a whole in dynastic China. Secular literature of all kinds was now first printed; the varied flood of printed books from this age was never to be excelled in beauty and technical perfection. State and private schools flourished, bibliographic study was pursued zealously, and Chinese libraries reached greater cumulative size than ever before.

Interrupted temporarily in the early twelfth century by a disastrous invasion (which led to the long alien occupation of northern China), these activities continued in the Southern Sung until the Mongol conquest of 1279. During this last century and a half the scholar, the printer, and the bibliophile were especially productive, and all three were stimulated by governmental action. The Southern Sung rulers maintained a cluster of scholarly agencies to further scholarly and literary development. Several were concerned especially with promoting education, with printing books and distributing them. Others were primarily engaged in compiling, writing, and editing works for government use or to benefit the nation at large.

The most important agency in the latter group was the Imperial Library (*Pi-shu sheng*), which came to play a vital role in state operations through scholarly research, through the administration of the largest collection of books and documents in Sung society, and finally through the use of its staff positions as a proving ground for promising officials destined to go on to posts in important policy-making organs. The role of the Imperial Library and its relation to the other scholarly agencies constitute the main theme of this book.

THE PURSUIT OF SCHOLARSHIP

The interest societies exhibit in the pursuit of scholarship, that is purposive inquiry, varies in style and in intensity within each one depending upon the era studied. Western Europe in the fifteenth century is a dramatic example of a society preoccupied with learning. It is, however, not the only era in which this society focused so intently on this activity. The pursuit of scholarship is known to have been a major concern in the twelfth century and still earlier in the eighth. Other societies, with the most varied interests and motivations, have at times shown a similarly intense interest in the promotion of knowledge.[1]

---

[1] For statements on aspects of this subject see Joseph Ben-David, *The Scientist's Role in Society: A Comparative Study*

Explanations of the varying intensity of scholarly activity may be found in the structure of the society studied.[2] In China the imperial government, with the emperor at its head and his household in close attendance, formed the apex of society. He ruled from an urbane capital city by means of an elaborate bureaucratic government staffed by a humanistically educated, and to a significant degree, a competitively selected corps of officials. It is this group in office and those informally associated with them that made the most significant contributions to scholarship. Powerful merchants, considerably lower in social standing, occasionally challenged their position, but with only limited success. The bulk of the population consisted of farming households, for the most part located in small villages throughout the extensive land empire. Artisans worked in close proximity to all social groups.[3] It is the relationship of government to the scholar and the works he generated which are our objects of concern.

THE CANON OF ORTHODOX BELIEF

It has been suggested that a society is sustained to a degree by the cluster of ideas forming for each one its canon of orthodox belief. Specific institutions are the bearers of these ideas. A non-literate society passes them on as part of the oral tradition, whereas a literate society tends to rely on the written text to transmit this canon.[4] In Western Europe, Christian ideas long provided the content of orthodoxy and the Christian church transmitted them. The Bible, of course, was the canon. In other societies the pattern has varied, but the basic functions remain the same.

The canon of orthodox belief in Chinese society of the early imperial era consisted of five works associated with the Confucian tradition. These were the *Book of History (Shu ching)*, a collection of documents; the *Book of Poetry (Shih ching)*, a collection of poems and songs; the *Book of Rites (Li chi)*, a guide to court ritual; the *Spring and Autumn Annals (Ch'un-ch'iu)*, a chronicle of the state of Lu for the years 722–481 B.C. and the *Book of Changes (I ching)*, a divination manual.[5] These served as the touchstones for governmental principles, which came to stress above

all the humanistic point of view advanced by Confucius (551–479 B.C.) and perpetuated by his followers. A significant difference from Western Europe, however, was that in imperial China the government was the most important institutional guardian of the canon. Furthermore, and perhaps for other reasons as well, Chinese tradition placed a high value on the pursuit of scholarship. Consequently, the government from the Han period (206 B.C.–220 A.D.) onward patronized all scholarly activity enthusiastically, but canonical scholarship above all.[6]

The process of establishing the government as the bearer of orthodoxy and custodian of its texts extended over most of the former Han (206 B.C.–8 A.D.). This government completed the unification of China, a task which had been attempted unsuccessfully by its predecessor the Ch'in (221–207 B.C.). Successive emperors, almost without exception, fostered Confucian ideas. Emperor Kao (r. 206–194 B.C.), the first ruler of the Han, initially was hostile toward the Confucian point of view, but by the end of his reign he accepted many of its ideas. After a setback in the next two reigns Emperor Wen (r. 179–156 B.C.) assumed the throne and followed the lead of the first Han emperor, particularly by emphasizing written examinations for officials. A major step forward came with Emperor Wu (r. 140–87 B.C.), the youthful scholarly enthusiast, who sanctioned the establishment of a government school at the capital for training prospective civil service examinees. The curriculum of this school was built on the five Confucian works which were already moving toward canonical status. Moreover, the teachers in the school were Confucians.[7] Emperor Hsüan (r. 73–48 B.C.) exhibited an enthusiasm for Confucian ideas, and called scholars to the Shih-ch'ü Pavilion (*Shih Ch'ü Ko*)[8] to discuss canonical texts in 53 B.C. By the time his son Emperor Yüan (r. 48–33 B.C.) assumed the throne Confucian ideas were unchallenged. The five works most esteemed by the Confucians were accepted as authoritative canonical texts and the government assumed the responsibility for their interpretation.[9]

(Englewood Cliffs, 1971) and R. R. Bolgar, *The Classical Heritage and its Beneficiaries from the Carolingian Age to the End of the Renaissance* (New York, 1964).

[2] George C. Homans, "Bringing Men Back In," *Amer. Sociol. Rev.* 29 (1964): pp 809–818. See also Bernard Bailyn, *Education in the Forming of American Society* (Chapel Hill, 1960), pp. 3–49.

[3] Ch'ü T'ung-tsu, "Chinese Class Structure and its Ideology," *Chinese Thought and Institutions* (Chicago, 1957), pp. 235–250.

[4] E. R. Dodds, *The Greeks and the Irrational* (Berkeley, 1951), pp. 75–76.

[5] Translations of these and related texts with introductory essays and notes are conveniently available in James Legge (trans.), *The Chinese Classics* (5 v., London, 1865–1872).

[6] R. P. Kramers, "Conservatism and the Transmission of the Confucian Canon," *Jour. Oriental Studies* 2 (1966): p. 119.

[7] Tjan Tjoe-som (trans.), *Po Hu T'ung: The Comprehensive Discussion in the White Tiger Hall* (2 v., Leiden, 1949) 1: pp. 84–85. See also Burton Watson (trans.), *Records of the Grand Historian of China* (2 v., New York, 1961) 2: pp. 399–401 for the original memorial by Kung-Sun Hung.

[8] Tjan Tjoe-som (trans.), *Po Hu T'ung* 2: pp. 89–94 and 128–136.

[9] Homer H. Dubs (trans.), *The History of the Former Han Dynasty* (2 v., Baltimore, 1944) 2: pp. 341–351. See also Burton Watson (trans.), *Records of the Grand Historian of China* 2: pp. 395–412 for a translation of the document on which this interpretation is based and James Legge (trans.), *The Chinese Classics* 1: pp. 1–11. For specific instances of canonical re-interpretations see Walter Liebenthal (trans.), "Wang Pi's New Interpretation of the I CHING," *Harvard Jour. Asiatic Studies* 10 (1947): pp. 124–161 and R. P. Kra-

The adoption of the Confucian point of view is explained in part by the felt need of the government for internal peace. The long period of chaos which preceded the Han made leaders prone to foster unity, including ideological unity, to promote this peace. As a unifying ideology any fully accepted teaching might have served the purpose, but that of the Confucians was more acceptable in that its humanistic precepts encouraged a willing compliance on the part of all groups in society to the wishes of the government. Moreover, the Confucians as teachers of prospective officials were strategically placed to promote their ideas. Their position was strengthened when the written examination was instituted for prospective officials and further strengthened when the government established the school in the capital for the instruction of prospective civil service examinees.[10]

The study, authentication, and dissemination of Confucian writings thus became a governmental function. While the enforcement of an orthodox uniformity on doctrinal nuance concerned the government in the Sung far less than it once had the Han and again would the Ming (1368–1644) and the Ch'ing (1644–1911), the establishment and dissemination of accurate texts was important to the Sung. The scholarly agencies of the government, chief among them the Imperial Library, assumed the responsibility for this task.

DOCUMENT COMPILATION AND HISTORIOGRAPHY

From early times, the keeping of historical records called forth an interest on the part of Chinese rulers and their literate officials scarcely inferior to that exhibited in recovering and preserving the canonical writings. Two works of the canon, the *Book of History* and the *Spring and Autumn Annals,* were indeed (to differing degrees) historical compilations.

In the course of centuries the actual attention devoted to history grew steadily, and by the Sung dynasty the historical enterprise certainly exceeded canonical scholarship in the magnitude of activities involved. History provided examples to follow or avoid in governmental policy, touching on concerns ranging from imperial patterns of life and the recruitment and training of officials to tax assessment, the management of currency, and foreign affairs. Its lessons were discussed in seminars before the emperors.

The most significant historical work in the early imperial period is the *Historical Records (Shih chi),* largely compiled around 100 B.C. by an official, Ssu-Ma Ch'ien, as an extracurricular activity. To compile the

work he used governmental libraries and archives. His work became the model for the standard histories (*cheng-shih*), the core of Chinese historiography, which were compiled from the seventh century onward by each ruling government for its predecessor. Not only did the government commission these histories, but its agencies also compiled the works on which they were based. Historical writing became the major activity of the Imperial Library and the associated scholarly agencies.

Officials appointed to positions in other agencies were responsible for compiling minutes of court and ministerial meetings. Subsequently these were edited and compiled by the scholarly agencies into works which were consulted in conjunction with agency archives to produce a variety of histories. As these evolved over the centuries, the most notable came to be the "reign chronicles" (*shih-lu*) and the "reign histories" (*kuo-shih*). In addition, a number of other compilations were produced such as the "selected documents" (*hui-yao*) and collections of imperial writings.[11] Government historiographical work was not only an official enterprise; it also became the basis for much of private historical scholarship in that government works circulated among the literate. In addition the government concerned itself to a lesser degree with many other subjects as well as the encyclopedias which began to be available. These works found their way into numerous private libraries by means of hand-copying. After the fall of the T'ang (618–906) the increasingly widespread use of wood block-printing aided this process.[12]

LIBRARIES AND ARCHIVES

The government maintained libraries and archives as a necessary adjunct to scholarship and the conduct of

mers, "Conservatism and the Transmission of the Confucian Canon," pp. 119–132.

[10] Homer H. Dubs (trans.), *The History of the Former Han Dynasty* 2: pp. 351–353. See also Hu Shih, "The Establishment of Confucianism as a State Religion during the Han Dynasty," *Jour. North China Branch of the Royal Asiatic Soc.* **60** (1929): pp. 20–41.

[11] A succinct summary of the subject may be found in Edwin G. Pulleyblank, "The Historiographical Tradition," in Raymond Dawson (ed.), *The Legacy of China* (Oxford, 1964), pp. 143–164.

[12] Yeh Meng-te, *Shih-lin yen-yü* (in *Pai-hai,* 1573–1620), 8/5b–7a comments on the spread of printing in several essays. Hereafter cited as *SLYY*. For a bibliographic note on this work see Robert des Rotours (trans.), *Traité des Fonctionnaires et Traité de l'Armée, traduits de la Nouvelle Histoire des T'ang* (2 v., Leiden, 1947). As early as 994 the newly collated *Shih chi, Han shu,* and *Hou Han shu* were cut in Hangchou and transported to the Directorate of Education (*Kuo-tzu chien*). See *Sung hui-yao chi-kao* (Taipei, 1967), *ch'ung-ju* 4/1a. Hereafter cited as *SHY:CJ*. See also Ch'eng Chü, *Lin-t'ai ku-shih* (in: *Shih-wan chüan lou ts'ung-shu,* 1879), 2/9b–10a. Hereafter cited as *LTKS*. Later on the Southern Sung printing blocks were cut in Szechwan for the *Kuo-ch'ao hui-yao ts'ung-lei* and similarly placed in the Directorate of Education. See Ma Tuan-lin, *Wen-hsien t'ung-k'ao* (1859), 201/14b. Hereafter cited as *TK*. See also Ch'en Chen-sung, *Chih-chai shu-lu chieh-t'i* (Chiang-su, 1883), 5/31b. Hereafter cited as *SLCT*. The first project was 300 *chüan* in length and the latter 588 *chüan,* suggesting the size to which wood block-printed books could run.

official business almost from its inception. Indeed books were readily available in the era of Confucius.[13] With the formation of the imperial government the tradition was continued and in successive centuries enlarged.

In the third century B.C. the Ch'in dynasty, while extremely wary of views which did not correspond to its own and inclined to suppress certain works, still found it necessary to maintain at least limited collections and to permit books on some subjects to circulate freely in the empire. Moreover, as the regime controlled China for only a scant decade and one-half, its antagonistic policy toward disapproved books was probably not entirely effective. The upheavals at the end of the regime were much more injurious to the extant body of recorded knowledge. Except for certain documents the governmental collections were probably completely destroyed in the debacle.[14]

The dynastic government of Han did not inherit an abundance of books from its predecessor. As noted above this was due less to the proscription of certain works by the government, than to the destruction of books by fire and pillage in the fighting which accompanied the fall of the Ch'in. Liu Pang, the founder of the Han, sacked the Ch'in capital of Hsien-yang in 206 B.C. and it is said that the fires in which the governmental collections were consumed burned for three months.[15] The Han government, however, became an outstanding conservator of documents and scholarly works. Emperor Wu is credited with the establishment of the governmental libraries in which a considerable number of titles were gathered and organized for use. Pan Ku, author of the *History of the Former Han Dynasty* (*Han shu*), a work written around 100, noted that Emperor Wu formulated a plan for libraries in the government. He appointed officials to transcribe various scholarly works so that they might be placed in these libraries.[16]

The subsequent growth of governmental collections in the Han was due in large part to the existence of private libraries from which they could draw desired items. Commissioners were sent throughout the empire in search of works. Library owners who would not contribute texts were persuaded to allow the government to arrange to make copies. Kung-Sun Hung, a high official under Emperor Wu, is credited with carrying out one of the most successful of these campaigns to gather works from private sources.[17]

Another significant development occurred after the reign of Emperor Wu. Liu Hsiang (*ca.* 80–8 B.C.) was placed at the head of a commission to examine works in governmental collections. The members of this commission would emend a work, the contents of which Liu Hsiang would then summarize before presenting it along with a summary to the emperor. The annotated bibliography which grew out of this process, the *Separate Records* (*Pieh lu*), was the first of many to be produced in imperial China. Liu Hsiang died in 8 B.C., but his son Liu Hsin continued the scholarly work in the governmental libraries begun by his father. He arranged the writings of this collection into seven classes thereby carrying out the first classification and descriptive cataloging project in China.[18]

Civil strife in the latter part of the second century brought the Han government to an end early in the third, severely disrupting all its efforts to maintain collections of books. When in 190 Emperor Hsien moved the capital to avoid battle, most of the governmental holdings were lost. For almost the next four centuries no single ruler controlled the whole empire; nevertheless, each government acknowledged its obligation toward the conservation of scholarship, making an effort appropriate to the resources at its command.[19]

With the reunification of the empire toward the end of the sixth century the government once again began a long and a fruitful drive to foster learning and conserve scholarship. The first Sui ruler, Emperor Wen (r. 589–604), actively encouraged people to contribute works to governmental libraries. In his reign a modest number of titles were acquired. His son and successor, Emperor Yang (r. 605–618), accelerated the gathering of texts, and brought together a sizable collection.[20] As a ruler he was less successful, and after a series of rebellions his dynasty was supplanted in 618 by the new and more enduring house of T'ang.

The T'ang government began to gather items for its collections almost from the outset. In 621 the massive holdings of an independent kingdom subdued by governmental armies were transported to the capital. Despite losses en route this acquisition added a substantial number of texts to the governmental libraries. In the decades that followed, these were supplemented by acquiring or copying works from private library owners. Inducements were offered in the form of cash and silk. This practice, no doubt combined with other more subtle inducements to donors, added materially to the size and quality of the state libraries. Before the middle of the eighth century these libraries contained as many as 53,915 *chüan* of older works, exclusive of duplicates, plus 28,469 *chüan* of contemporary authors.

[13] H. G. Creel, *Studies in Early Chinese Culture* (Baltimore, 1937), pp. 21–48.
[14] Wu Kwang-tsing, "Libraries and Book Collecting in China Before the Invention of Printing," *T'ien Hsia Monthly* **5** (1937): pp. 241–242.
[15] *Ibid.*, pp. 241–242.
[16] Pan Ku, *Han shu*, 30/1b.
[17] Wu Kwang-tsing, "Libraries and Book Collecting in China before the Invention of Printing," p. 242.

[18] Tsien Tsuen-hsuin, *Written on Bamboo and Silk* (Chicago, 1962), p. 14.
[19] Wu Kwang-tsing, "Libraries and Book Collecting in China before the Invention of Printing," pp. 245–253.
[20] *Ibid.*, pp. 253–257.

These two combined must have constituted a notable collection.[21]

Government holdings suffered severe losses in the rebellion of An Lu-shan which broke out in 755.[22] Yet, in keeping with tradition, as soon as the fighting subsided an effort was made to restore the library holdings to their former state. The campaign was successful and by the beginning of the ninth century the building accommodations were being taxed by the continual stream of new acquisitions.[23] The ill-fated collections were destroyed once more during the Huang Ch'ao rebellion which began in 880.[24] Although efforts were made to reconstitute the collections again, the T'ang was near its end and considerably fewer works were gathered now than in the middle of the eighth century and the early ninth.[25]

The periodic destruction of the T'ang governmental collections and their subsequent reconstitution had precedent in earlier periods, but a new development was becoming apparent in the seventh and eighth centuries, that is, the emergence of the Imperial Library. Whereas several library collections existed in the Han government without any evidence of unity or separate and clearly distinguishable functions, by the seventh and eighth centuries there was a discernible grouping of libraries for the use of officials and other scholars.[26]

Within the Sung government the distinction is clear between the palace libraries, the Imperial Library, and the small book collections located in various govern-

TABLE 1

REPOSITORIES FOR SUNG IMPERIAL PAPERS[a]

Emperor	Reigned	Repository	Founded
T'ai Tsu	960/ 1– 976/10[b]		
T'ai Tsung	976/10– 997/3	Lung T'u Ko	1008–1017[c]
Chen Tsung	997/ 3–1022/2	T'ien Chang Ko	1022
Jen Tsung	1022/ 2–1063/4	Pao Wen Ko	1063
Ying Tsung	1063/ 4–1067/1		
Shen Tsung	1067/ 1–1085/3	Hsien Mu Ko	1086
Che Tsung	1085/ 3–1100/1	Hui Yu Ko	1108
Hui Tsung	1100/ 1–1125/12	Fu Wen Ko	1140/5
Ch'in Tsung	1125/12–1127/5		
Kao Tsung	1127/ 5–1162/6	Huan Chang Ko	1188/10
Hsiao Tsung	1162/ 6–1189/2	Hua Wen Ko	1196/5
Kuang Tsung	1189/ 2–1194/7	Pao Mu Ko	1202/11
Ning Tsung	1194/ 7–1224/8[d]	Pao Chang Ko	1226/10
Li Tsung	1224/ 8–1264/10	Hsien Wen Ko	1265/6
Tu Tsung	1264/10–1274/7		
Kung Tsung	1274/ 7–1276/5		
Tuan Tsung	1276/ 5–1278/4		
Ti Ping	1278/ 4–1279/3		

[a] Data drawn from Ch'ien Yüeh-yu, *Hsien ch'un Lin an chih* (Ch'ien t'ang chu shih, 1830), 2/1a–4b. Hereafter cited as *LAC(3)*. *TK* 54/22a–25a gives the same information except for omission of the last imperial repository, the *Hsien Wen Ko*.

[b] Number following year indicates lunar month.

[c] Founded in the beginning of the period 1008–1017.

[d] Intercalary 8th month.

ment offices. The palace libraries were located in the palace grounds (*ta-nei*), an enclosed area of the capital reserved for the emperor. They served as a means of relaxation for the emperor. Customarily he would invite several officials to a banquet in the palace grounds after which they might go to one of the palace libraries to examine its collection. On one occasion the emperor is said to have held the catalog of the library collection while an attendant brought forward the works he requested for examination by his party.[27] Little scholarly work appears to have been done in these libraries. When the texts were in need of collation, personnel from the Imperial Library and the several associated scholarly agencies were called upon to do it.[28]

Among the palace libraries was a group of repositories for imperial papers (see table 1). A Sung tradition called for an emperor to establish a repository for his predecessor's writings. This resulted in eleven Sung imperial repositories. The exceptions were Emperors T'ai Tsu and Ying Tsung for whom no papers remained.[29] Emperor Ch'in Tsung, who served only fifteen months on the throne before he was captured by the Jurchen and carried north, and the four rulers who during the last fifteen years of the Southern Sung spent their reigns as fugitives from the Mongols.

---

[21] Robert des Rotours (trans.), *Traité des Functionnaires* 1: p. 191, n. 2. See also Thomas F. Carter, *The Invention of Printing and its Spread Westward* (rev. ed., New York, 1955), pp. 42–43, n. 1. Both of these notes also point to the difficulties one encounters in the interpretation of figures for the sizes of actual library collections. One major problem is the meaning of the word *chüan*. Over the course of the millennium from the Han through the Sung the Chinese book evolved from the *chüan* (roll) to the *ts'e* (volume), a flat unit often smaller than its Western counterpart, but perhaps as ample in content given the conciseness of the language in which it was written. Several rolls might be arranged as pages and bound into a volume. In this manner the roll became a literary division within a book. Despite this transition in the form of the book the Chinese bibliographer continued to describe a complete work and a library collection by the number of *chüan* it contained, seldom indicating whether it was a roll or a literary division within a volume.

[22] Robert des Rotours (trans.), *Histoire de Ngan Lou-chan* (Paris, 1962), pp. 167–211.

[23] Wu Kwang-tsing, "Scholarship, Book Production and Libraries in China, 618–1644" (unpublished Ph.D. dissertation, University of Chicago, 1944), p. 81.

[24] Howard S. Levy (trans.), *Biography of Huang Ch'ao* (Berkeley, 1961), pp. 1–7.

[25] Wu Kwang-tsing, "Scholarship, Book Production and Libraries in China," pp. 82–83.

[26] *Ibid.*, p. 84. At one point in the middle of the T'ang, the *Chi Hsien Tien Shu-yüan*, one of the palace libraries contained 25,961 *chüan* in its main collection (*ssu-pu*) and the Imperial Library 31,085 *chüan*. See Robert des Rotours (trans.), *Traité des Functionnaires* 1: p. 191, n. 2 and p. 206, n. 4.

[27] Wang Ying-lin, *Yü hai* (1883), 164/19a–20b. Hereafter cited as *YH*.

[28] *LTKS* 2/8b–9a.

[29] *YH* 163/20b.

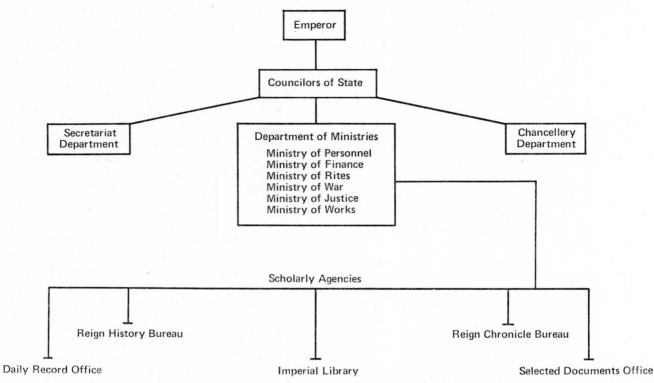

FIG. 1. Scholarly agencies within the structure of the Sung government after 1082. Adapted from Edward A. Kracke, Jr., *Translation of Sung Civil Service Titles,* chart II, "The Sung Central Government after about 1080."

With the establishment of each repository went three honorary titles: Academician (*Hsüeh-shih*), Auxiliary-academician (*Chih-hsüeh-shih*), and Academician-in-waiting (*Tai-chih*). These were conferred on councilors or other high officials.[30] Thus an official might receive the title of Academician of the Lung T'u Pavilion (*Lung-t'u ko hsüeh-shih*), the repository for Emperor T'ai Tsung's writings, or Academician-in-waiting of the T'ien Chang Pavilion (*T'ien-chang ko tai-chih*), the repository for Emperor Chen Tsung's writings.

The Imperial Library, a separate agency serving the needs of government and scholars engaged in their own studies, was functionally existent from the beginning of the Sung, but formally re-instituted in its distinctive Sung pattern as an agency of the government only in 1082. After that year it was the most significant member of the group of scholarly agencies in the central government engaged primarily in textual collation, document compilation and history writing. Imperial Library personnel were in charge of the compilation of the "daily record" (*jih-li*), a collection of governmental documents arranged in chronological order and out of which material was drawn for several other types of works. One of these, the "selected documents," was another type of work compiled by Imperial Library

personnel who filled positions in the Daily Record Office (*Jih-li so*) and the Selected Documents Office (*Hui-yao so*), the second and third of the scholarly agencies, on a concurrent basis. The fourth, the Reign Chronicle Bureau (*Shih-lu yüan*), compiled the "reign chronicle" and the fifth, the Reign History Bureau (*Kuo-shih yüan*), compiled the "reign history" (see fig. 1).

In addition to serving as the most notable scholarly agency the Imperial Library maintained the largest collection of books and documents in the government for the use of officials and others. The associated scholarly agencies were dependent on these collections to fulfill their assigned functions. Through the course of the Sung the Imperial Library collections grew to great size, although they were destroyed several times. Its holdings were burned in 1015 after over half a century of growth.[31] In keeping with tradition they were quickly reconstituted, only to be carried off by the Jurchen invaders from Manchuria in 1127. New collections were brought together again in the early years of the Southern Sung. They grew in number until 1231 when they too were consumed by fire.[32] We do not know whether the collections were completely reconstituted. Perhaps the Mongol presence

---

[30] Edward A. Kracke, Jr., *Civil Service in Early Sung China, 960–1067* (Cambridge, 1963), p. 33, n. 19 and p. 80.

[31] *LTKS* 2/5b–6b.

[32] *Nan Sung kuan-ho hsü-lu* (in: *Wu-lin ch'ang-ku ts'ung-pien,* 1886), 2/1b–2a. Hereafter cited as NSKKL(2).

on the northern border was already of sufficient concern to direct the attention of the government to defense, leaving the Imperial Library with a minimum of resources with which to work.

There is evidence to suggest that many, if not all, governmental agencies, also maintained small collections of books. In this case the library was evidently an aid to the conduct of official business. For instance in 1133 the Secretariat Department (*Chung-shu sheng*) and the Chancellery Department (*Men-hsia sheng*) received a copy of the *Cheng-ho ch'ung-hsiu kuo-ch'ao hui-yao,* one of the compilations of "selected documents," for their use.[33] In what appears to have been a normal request, the Court of Imperial Sacrifices (*T'ai-ch'ang ssu*) also requested a number of books of rites for its collection.[34] These agency libraries appear to have been small, undoubtedly just sufficient for the conduct of official business.

As noted above, the size and quality of the Imperial Library collections appear to have increased steadily through the Sung at K'ai-feng, its northern seat, until they were carried off by the Jurchen in 1127. Texts which were systematically gathered from the empire were first checked for accuracy and completeness and then placed in the appropriate cabinet for use. Early in the twelfth century, however, the enemy which appeared on the northern border deprived the Sung of its capital at K'ai-feng and with it the holdings of the Imperial Library. These Jurchen tribesmen were one of many such invading groups who raided the empire through the course of Chinese history.

Tribes from the steppe who were skilled in archery and horsemanship menaced China in spite of persistent efforts of the government to incorporate them into a tributary system and manage them as vassals. Martial by nature and driven periodically by a shortage of food, they often raided the northern border, at times invaded China proper, and for almost a century after the Sung even ruled the empire as they would again three centuries later. The area along the northern border where the tilled field gave way to the steppe or the forest was the line of separation between two largely incompatible ways of life. When the government was strong it could usually repel the invaders. Yet in spite of internal unity in the Sung, the formidable military machines built up in the north overcame all its defenses.[35]

The earliest of the chief contenders for power on the northern border during the Sung were the Khitan tribes who occupied the area to the northeast of China and established the Liao dynasty (947–1125). As early as 907 the Khitan had formed a tribal confederation, similar to the one earlier organized by the Hsiung-nu, under the leadership of Yeh-lü A-pao-chi (872–926). They had gradually acquired literacy and technology with the assistance of talented Chinese emigrants. Moreover, their management of material resources and well-trained cavalry were effective means for expanding their area of control. By 947 the Khitan had extended their sway to the line of the Great Wall and to sixteen prefectures southward of it.

During the ensuing century and a half the Khitan lived sometimes at war with their Chinese neighbors, sometimes at peace, but ever extending their borrowings from Chinese culture and technology. The Tangut people on China's northwestern frontiers, growing in power and danger from the later years of the tenth century, proceeded similarly to borrow from the Chinese heritage.

A more formidable danger arose in the early twelfth century when the Jurchen, a vassal people of the Khitan, rebelled against their former overlords in 1114 under the outstanding leadership of A-ku-ta. These people developed a military power unprecedented in East Asia. The Sung, in another effort to regain the sixteen provinces lost earlier, allied themselves with the Jurchen in 1120 against the Khitan. The power of the latter collapsed two years later under the relentless attack of the Jurchen and by 1125 the Khitan were completely vanquished. In the peace settlement which followed, the Jurchen turned over only six of the sixteen prefectures sought by the Sung. The government balked at this. In response the Jurchen carried their invasion south into Sung territory, sweeping through all of north China. Emperor Hui Tsung abdicated in 1125, but his son and successor, Emperor Ch'in Tsung, had no better success in holding back the invaders. The Jurchen occupied the Sung capital of K'ai-feng in 1126 and in the next year plunged south of the Yangtze River. South China, however, was unsuitable terrain for the Jurchen to operate in and they were eventually forced to withdraw. The border between the two antagonists stabilized along the Huai River. Finally in 1141 a peace treaty was signed by the two contenders.[36]

On capturing K'ai-feng in 1126 the Jurchen were eager to acquire still further accouterments of Chinese civilization, including the collections of the Imperial Library and the printing blocks from the Directorate of Education. These were carried off by the invaders in 1127 along with the holdings of the T'ai Ch'ing Library (*T'ai Ch'ing Lou*), one of the palace libraries. The number of works obtained by the Jurchen from these sources is unknown.[37]

[33] *SHY:CJ* 4/23a–23b.

[34] *SHY:CJ* 4/21a–21b.

[35] Edwin O. Reischauer and John K. Fairbank, *A History of East Asian Civilization* (2 v., Boston, 1960) 1: pp. 243–249. Yü Ying-shih, *Trade and Expansion in Han China* (Berkeley, 1967), pp. 40–51.

[36] *Ibid.,* pp. 196–197 and 208–211.

[37] *Ching-k'ang yao-lu* (in: *Shih-wan chüan lou ts'ung-shu,* 1830), 15/17a; 15/19a; 15/23a; 15/23b. Numerous comments in Southern Sung sources lament the loss of the Northern Sung Imperial Library collections. See, for example, *SHY:CJ* 4/25b. Ma Tuan-lin estimated that four or five

In addition to occupying K'ai-feng and taking custody of the Imperial Library holdings, the Jurchen captured former Emperor Hui Tsung and Emperor Ch'in Tsung and removed them to the steppe. Another son of Emperor Hui Tsung, posthumously titled Kao Tsung, assumed the throne (r. 1127–1162) and, withdrawing his administrative seat to south China, continued the dynasty, thereafter known as the Southern Sung.

Emperor Kao Tsung situated himself in the area south of the Yangtze River near the seacoast. He moved about in the ensuing decade as the need arose, but seldom beyond the borders of the two adjoining Liang-che circuits (*Liang-che-tung* and *Liang-che-hsi*). His movements appear to have been dictated by the military operations of Jurchen armies. Early in the summer of 1127 the emperor was located near the city of Nan-ching just south of the Yangtze River.[38] Two years later he was to be found farther south in Hang-chou. He returned to Nan-ching in that same year (1129), but remained there for only several months before moving south again.[39] The emperor apparently stayed there, making one trip of which we are certain west of the Che River, until the latter part of 1131 when he set out for Hang-chou again. He arrived there early in 1132.[40] From this point on Hang-chou seems to have housed the central administration, although at times the emperor still traveled as far north as the south bank of the Yangtze River.[41]

The loss of the Imperial Library collections in 1127 was a severe blow to the government, but the nadir was reached in 1129 when the emperor temporarily abolished it. It was re-activated in 1131 in the prefecture of Shao-hsing.[42] Here the Imperial Library was housed in two buildings belonging to a certain Sun family.[43] After moving to Hang-chou in 1132 it was housed briefly in a building belonging to a certain Sung family before being established at Fa Hui Temple (*Fa Hui Ssu*). This too was a temporary site for the Imperial Library and associated scholarly agencies. Twelve years later they would move into a building complex designed and built especially for their use.

II. BUILDINGS AND GROUNDS

The principal scholarly agencies were housed in the well-integrated Imperial Library building complex built especially for that purpose in the capital city of Hang-chou in 1143–1144. It was within easy reach of the palace grounds and other major agencies of the government. In the manner of traditional Chinese architecture, buildings were arranged symmetrically within a narrow walled enclosure. In the case of the Imperial Library an addition was built onto the lower east side in 1145 to house the Reign History Bureau. There were four functional areas in this building complex: the Imperial Library area, the compilation and history area, the rest and contemplation area, and the service area.

CAPITAL CITY OF HANG-CHOU

After moving about the area south of the Yangtze River for several years, the emperor settled the government in the city of Hang-chou in 1132. The city was officially designated the temporary capital of the Southern Sung in 1138 and only three years later the government concluded a peace treaty with the Jurchen which recognized the Huai River as the border.[1] Famous as a picturesque city and a great commercial center, Hang-chou quickly grew in population to about one million persons, to become the center of Southern Sung society. It was then as now situated on the south side of the Shanghai promontory, a portion of the Yangtze River delta. On the south and east flowed the Che River and to the west was the shallow West Lake (*Hsi-hu*). Thus, as a capital city, it was both strategically and pleasantly located.

Hang-chou, the former provincial capital and terminus of the grand canal, was rebuilt in part to suit it to its new role as the capital of the empire. Its surrounding inner wall, estimated at eleven miles in length with thirteen gates, allowed people and goods to move in and out conveniently. Five additional gates accommodated the flow of water and water traffic in this canal-laced city. Artfully designed bridges, in most cases made of stone, spanned the canals at numerous places.[2]

The palace grounds, surrounded by a wall of its own, was laid out on a low-lying hill on the south end of the city. Elaborately decorated buildings set in this park were reserved for the exclusive use of the emperor and his entourage. The palace grounds of the latter part of the Southern Sung are described by Marco Polo who based his description on the comments of a merchant who gave him a tour of the area which had

Northern Sung works out of ten were lost in the move south. This is in contrast to his estimated one or two out of ten lost in the period 1131–1225. See *TK* 174/38b.

[38] *Sung hui-yao chi-kao* (Taipei, 1967), *fang-yü* 2/3a. Hereafter cited as *SHY:FYü*.

[39] *LAC*(3) 1/10; 1/11a; *SHY:FYü* 2/7a.

[40] *LAC*(3) 1/11a–11b.

[41] *LAC*(3) 1/11b–12a; 1/13a, 1136, P'ing-chiang; 1/13a, 1137, Chien-K'ang. For a brief administrative history of Hang-chou and its environs see *LAC*(3) 2/1a–2b.

[42] *Sung hui-yao chi-kao* (Taipei, 1967), *chih-kuan* 18/24b. Hereafter cited as *SHY:CK*. See also *YH* 127/23b.

[43] Ch'en K'uei, *Nan Sung kuan-ko lu* (in: *Wu-lin ch'ang-ku ts'ung-pien*, 1886), 2/1a. Hereafter cited as *NSKKL* (1).

[1] *SHY:FYü* 2/3a.

[2] A. C. Moule, *Quinsai, with Other Notes on Marco Polo* (Cambridge, 1957), pp. 13–51, discusses the major physical features of the city of Hang-chou.

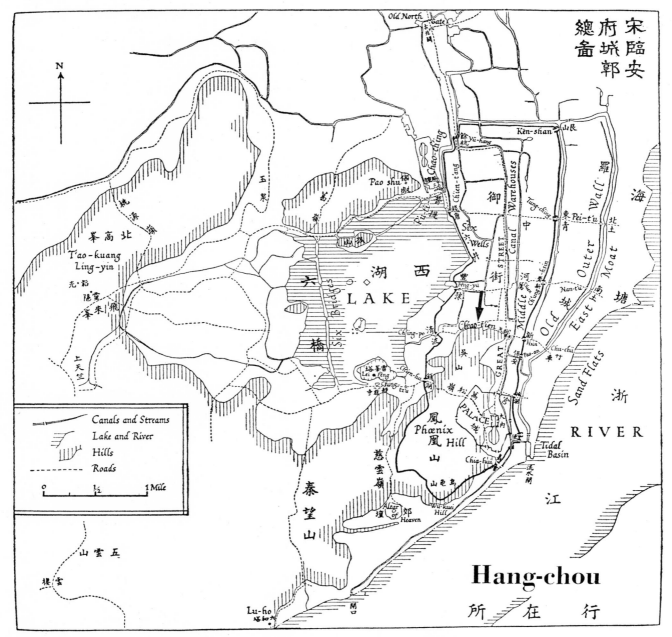

Fig. 2. Thirteenth-century Hang-chou and environs. Arrow indicates the approximate location of the Imperial Library building complex. Adapted from A. C. Moule, *Quinsai, with Other Notes on Marco Polo* (Cambridge, 1957), fig. 1.

not been cared for since the last days of the 1270's. He says in part,

In this city [of Hang-chou] . . . is the most beautiful and splendid palace in the world. No words of mine could describe its superlative magnificence, but I will briefly relate some of its main features. You must know that the king's predecessors had enclosed a space of land some ten miles in circumference with lofty battlemented walls and divided into three parts. The middle part was entered through a wide gateway flanked by pavilions of vast dimensions standing at ground level with their roofs sup-

ported by columns painted and wrought in fine gold and azure. Ahead was seen the largest and most important of these pavilions, similarly adorned with paintings and with gilded columns, and the ceiling gorgeously embellished with gold. On the inner walls were pictures of beasts and birds, knights and ladies, and scenes from the history of past kings, portrayed with consummate artistry. On every wall and every ceiling nothing met the eye but a blaze of gold and brilliant color.[3]

---

[3] Ronald Latham (trans.), *The Travels of Marco Polo* (Baltimore, 1958), pp. 196–197.

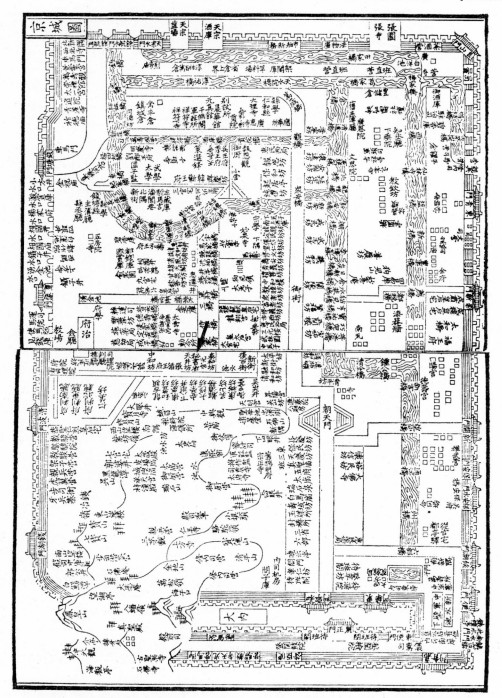

FIG. 3. Thirteenth-century Hang-chou. Arrow indicates the location of the Imperial Library building complex. Adapted from A. C. Moule, *Quinsai, with Other Notes on Marco Polo* (Cambridge, 1957), fig. 4.

Numerous smaller buildings were located on the grounds, often to take advantage of the view.

The main thoroughfare, three miles in length and paved with stone, ran north from the palace grounds almost to the other end of the city. Major agencies of the government were located on the west side of this thoroughfare within easy reach of the palace. Also several governmental agencies which dealt with the affairs of the imperial household were situated in this area. Each of these was housed in its own building complex, perhaps much like the one provided for the Imperial Library and associated scholarly agencies which we will describe below in detail.

IMPERIAL LIBRARY BUILDING COMPLEX

In response to a request by the Executive-assistant of the Imperial Library (*Pi-shu ch'eng*), Yen I in 1143, two years after peace was established with the Jurchen, Emperor Kao Tsung directed the fiscal intendants of the Liang-che circuits to undertake the construction of permanent quarters for the Imperial Library and associated scholarly agencies (see figs. 3, 7, and 8). The new building complex was completed in the following year amid an elaborate ceremony which included the emperor and a number of high officials. This remained the permanent quarters of the scholarly agencies until it burned down in 1231, presumably with the entire book collection, which may explain its complete absence from our libraries today.[4] One addition to this complex was made in 1145, that of the Reign History Bureau. It was a lesser complex of buildings built on to the lower east side of the original one.[5]

The Imperial Library building complex, exclusive of the Reign History Bureau, was enclosed within a wall 1,000 feet long and 190 feet wide (see Figs. 4, 7, and 8). The wall provided a measure of privacy and security in the midst of a bustling urban center. This narrow rectangular enclosure, arranged along a north–south axis, had an area of four and two-fifths acres. A narrow road twenty-five feet wide, originally conceived of as a fire lane, girded the outside of the wall; however, its effectiveness was impaired by the people who constantly encroached upon it, perhaps with living quarters and stalls for selling goods and services.[6]

Two other building complexes bordered the Imperial Library, one to the east and one to the west. The road mentioned above separated them from each other. On the south, the Imperial Library faced a main

thoroughfare also lined with building complexes, presumably carrying on governmental activities. The scholarly agencies were centrally located within the section of the city which was largely given over to governmental operations. It was within easy reach of the palace grounds to the south and of agencies such as the Directorate of Education to the north.[7]

IMPERIAL LIBRARY AREA

The whole Imperial Library building complex was laid out symmetrically with four discernible functional areas. The first of these was the Imperial Library area which dominated the complex; the second was the compilation and history area made up of two parts, the Compilation Hall (*Chu Tso T'ing*) and the Reign History Bureau; the third was the rest and contemplation area at the north end and the fourth was a service area at the south end.

The portion of the building complex given over to the Imperial Library operations began slightly north of the service area, but included the main gate. This was the core group of buildings within the building complex. In a traditional manner it consisted of two parts. The first of these was a central axis made up of three main southward facing buildings which were primarily used for ceremonies.[8]

The first of the three buildings was the Yu Wen Audience Hall (*Yu Wen Tien*). In front it had a gate three modules wide.[9] Passing through the gate one entered the five-module Yu Wen Audience Hall inside of which were a desk and chair arranged on a thick yellow silk rug for the emperor.[10] This was an audience hall, perhaps serving no other function than to accommodate the emperor on his occasional visits.

North of the Yu Wen Audience Hall stood the Imperial Archives building. It was the most imposing structure within the Imperial Library building complex. Although just as wide as the Yu Wen Audience Hall, it was a two-story structure, slightly more than forty feet high. The first floor served as a reception hall. It was furnished in exactly the same manner as the Yu Wen Audience Hall with a desk and chair set on a thick yellow silk rug for the emperor. Here he inspected the writings in the Imperial Archives collection which were partially housed on its second floor and partially in the two lateral buildings which were perpendicular to the main axis on its east and west

---

[4] *NSKKL*(1) 2/1b–2a; *SHY:CK* 18/27a. Similar problems were encountered in housing the Northern Sung imperial library collections. Initially they were put in the West Hall (*Hsi Kuan*), a small building. In 977 the Ch'ung Wen Library (*Ch'ung Wen Yüan*) was built to house the Chao Wen Institute (*Chao Wen Kuan*), the Chi Hsien Library (*Chi Hsien Tien*) and the Institute of History (*Shih Kuan*). The Imperial Archives (*Pi Ko*) were added in 988. This building complex was destroyed by fire in 1015 and sixteen years passed before another one was built, perhaps because the collections had grown too large. See *SHY:CK* 18/1a, 18/47a, 18/50a; *LTKS* 1/2a, 2/5b, 4/1a–1b; *YH* 52/30b–32a; Sun Feng-chi, *Chih-kuan fen-chi* (in: *Ssu-k'u ch'üan-shu chen-pen*, 1934), 15/59a. Hereafter cited as *CKFC*.

[5] *YH* 165/34a; *SHY:CK* 18/1b; Chou Tsung, *Ch'ien-tao Lin-an chih* (in: *Wu-lin ch'ang-ku ts'ung-pien*, 1886), 1/3b–4a; hereafter cited as *LAC*(1); Shih O, *Ch'un-yu Lin-an chih* (in: *Wu-lin ch'ang-ku ts'ung-pien*, 1886), 7/1a–1b. Hereafter cited as *LAC*(2). See also figs. 4, 7, and 8.

[6] *NSKKL*(1) 2/1b–2a.

[7] *LAC*(3) 1/6b–7a.

[8] Osvald Siren, "Chinese Architecture," *Encyclopedia Britannica* (14th ed.) **5**: pp. 557–558.

[9] A module is a *chien*, that is, the space between four posts. In traditional Chinese architectural literature the number of modules along the front of a building was the convenient way to indicate its size. See Appendix I, "The Imperial Library Building Complex" for a discussion of several technical points on traditional Chinese architecture and Figs. 7 and 8 for graphic views of the Imperial Library building complex.

[10] *NSKKL*(1) 2/2a.

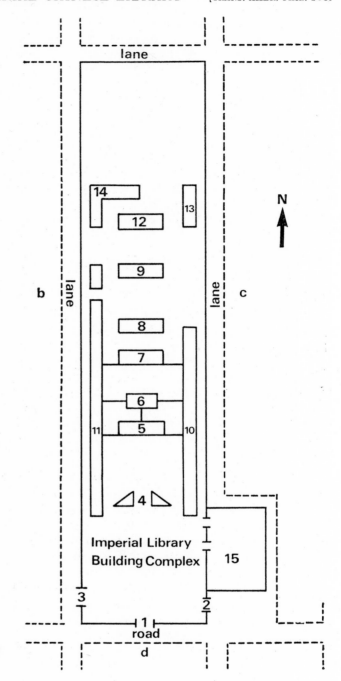

aGuide to the "Sketch Plan of the Imperial Library Building Complex":

1. Main Gate
2. East Side-gate
3. West Side-gate
4. Yu Wen Audience Hall Gate
5. Yu Wen Audience Hall
6. Pai Ko Platform
7. Imperial Archives
8. Pond
9. Tao Shan Assembly Hall
10. East Lateral Building
11. West Lateral Building
12. Compilation Hall
13. Daily Record Office
14. Selected Documents Office
15. Reign History Bureau

See also Figure 7, "Artist's Conception of the Imperial Library Building Complex" and Figure 8, "Detailed Plan of the Imperial Library Building Complex."

bT'ien Ching Building Complex (T'ien Ching Fang). It was formally called the T'ung Che Building Complex (T'ung Che Fang) according to LAC(2) 7/1b.

cCh'ing Ho Building Complex (Ch'ing Ho Fang).

dHuai Ch'ing Building Complex (Huai Ch'ing Fang).

FIG. 4. Sketch plan of the Imperial Library building complex. Based on *NSKKL*(1) 2/1b–8a.

sides. North of the Imperial Archives a pond fifty feet by fifteen, with a bridge crossing it, enhanced the landscape.[11]

The third building in this main central axis is the Tao Shan Assembly Hall (*Tao Shan T'ang*) for offi-

cial gatherings. Outside stood a bell and stanchion, perhaps to call meetings, and a number of tables and chairs. The *Pi-ko chu-k'u shu-mu*, a union catalog of Imperial Library holdings, was housed inside.[12] This location insured its security and still placed it within

[11] *NSKKL*(1) 2/2a–3a.

[12] *NSKKL*(1) 3/3a.

easy reach of the director (*Pi-shu chien*) and vice-director of the Imperial Library (*Pi-shu shao-chien*) whose offices were in the east and west ends of the Tao Shan Assembly Hall.

The ceremonial function of the first two buildings in this central axis is illustrated by the movements of the emperor and his party when he visited the Imperial Library on its official opening in 1144 and when the *Nan Sung kuan-ko lu* and accompanying *Chung-hsing kuan-ko shu-mu* were formally presented in 1178. On these two occasions the emperor and his entourage passed through the main gate and entered the Yu Wen Audience Hall. Here the emperor was the object of a felicitous ceremony. Afterwards everyone moved to the first floor of the Imperial Archives where they viewed writings of former emperors, paintings and calligraphy and antique bronze vessels. The whole party then returned to the Yu Wen Audience Hall for tea after which the emperor and his party departed.[13]

The buildings in the second part of the Imperial Library area, the two lateral buildings located perpendicularly to the main axis on its east and west sides, were given over largely to office space for personnel and depositories for the collections. The director and vice-director of the Imperial Library each occupied two module offices in the east and west ends of the Tao Shan Assembly Hall. This central location gave them ready access to all parts of the building complex and to the *Pi-ko chu-k'u shu-mu* also housed in the Tao Shan Assembly Hall. Furnishings suggest a functional office with some attention given to personal comfort. They include a black lacquered table, two chairs, and a small side bench. In addition, a low-lying couch was used for resting, a stand and basin for washing, and an oil brazier for making tea and warming food. Several screens served to divide the space according to taste.[14] The executive assistant of the Imperial Library had a two-module office in the north end of the east lateral building. His office was also furnished with a table, two chairs, and a side bench, plus a low-lying couch and an oil brazier and screens, but no mention is made of a wash basin or stand.[15] The offices of the remainder of the directive personnel were furnished similarly, suggesting a general uniformity in status in keeping with the slight differences in ranks.

Other Imperial Library operations were also carried out in the east and west lateral buildings which flanked the main axis of ceremonial buildings.

The librarians of the Imperial Library (*Pi-shu lang*) occupied three modules in the north end of the west lateral building. The center module appears to have been an entry or vestibule, while the other two were shared, one each by the two men who held the position of librarian.[16] The office space for collators (*Pi-shu sheng chiao-shu lang*) and correcting editors of the Imperial Library (*Pi-shu sheng cheng-tzu*) were slightly south of those for the executive assistant of the Imperial Library and the librarian. There were four offices of three modules each, two in the east lateral building and two in the west. Outside of each stood a sign board with the Rules for Collation written in full.[17] A kitchen was housed in the north end of the west lateral buildings,[18] a gravestone depository in the south end,[19] a bathroom and toilet in the north end of the east lateral building,[20] and a fire station in its south end.[21]

COMPILATION AND HISTORY AREA

The compilation of documents and the writing of history were carried on in two places; the cluster of buildings around the Compilation Hall and in the Reign History Bureau building complex. The Compilation Hall cluster was located north of the Imperial Library area. It was a natural continuation of the architectural plan of the Imperial Library. The Reign History Bureau on the other hand was added on to the lower east side in 1145, one year after the completion of the buildings in the original plan. Evidently the Compilation Hall cluster of buildings was not large enough to house the whole scholarly undertaking the government planned to carry out.

The Reign History Bureau was a well-integrated set of buildings, as well planned as the Imperial Library building complex to which it was attached. A plan similar to the Imperial Library area was followed, except that the main gate and the side gate were built into the west wall, giving personnel easy access to the larger unit. The main axis of buildings consisted of the Main Hall (*Cheng T'ing*) and the Reign History Hall (*T'ang*), the former containing the offices of the compilers (*Pien-hsiu kuan*) and the latter the offices of the intendant of the Reign History Bureau (*T'i-chü kuo-shih yüan*), the Reign History editors (*Hsiu kuo-shih*) and the associate Reign History editors (*T'ung-hsiu kuo-shih*). The lateral buildings on the east,

[13] For a description of a visit by the emperor in 1144 see *SHY:CK* 18/28a–29a, *YH* 27/17a, *NSKKL*(1) 6/1a–2b. For a description of a visit by the emperor in 1178 see *SHY:CK* 18/37b–42a, *NSKKL*(2) 6/1a–6b, *YH* 27/17a–17b.

[14] *NSKKL*(1) 2/3a. The intendant of the Imperial Library (*T'i-chü Pi-shu sheng*), an occasional appointee assigned to carry out special assignments, also had quarters within the Imperial Library building complex. These were west of the Yu Wen Audience Hall according to *LAC*(3) 7/17a. This is partially confirmed by the existence of the gateway to the intendant's quarters (*T'i Chü T'ing Chia Men*) west of the Yu Wen Audience Hall.

[15] *NSKKL*(1) 2/3b.

[16] *NSKKL*(1) 2/4a–4b.
[17] *NSKKL*(1) 2/3b, 2/4b.
[18] *NSKKL*(1) 2/4a.
[19] *NSKKL*(1) 2/3a.
[20] *NSKKL*(1) 2/5a.
[21] *NSKKL*(1) 2/4a.

south, and west sides provided space for utility rooms as well as offices for operative and service personnel.[22]

The Compilation Hall cluster, for the most part, housed the operation of those offices which carried on the compilation work for which the Imperial Library itself was responsible. First, the Compilation Hall. It housed the "diary of activity and repose" (*ch'i-chü chu*) and the "records of current government" (*shih-cheng chi*) which were the documents from which most of the material which went into the "daily record" were drawn. When finished, however, the latter documents were added to the Imperial Archives collections. In addition, the offices of the staff author (*Chu-tso lang*) and the assistant staff authors (*Chu-tso tso-lang*) who were in charge of the compilation of the "daily record" were located on the east and west sides of this building. The Compilation Hall also had a copy of the *Chu-tso shu-mu,* perhaps another working catalog of the Imperial Library collections. Outside of this building, too, stood a sign board with the Rules for Compilation written in full.[23]

On the east side of the Compilation Hall stood the Daily Record Office, a building of some nine modules given over primarily to activities in support of the compilation work. On the west side stood the Selected Documents Office in which the "selected documents" were compiled. In addition, it also housed several sets of printing blocks, including those for the *Nan Sung kuan-ko lu,* works not yet prepared for inclusion in the collections and duplicates and extraneous works.[24]

REST AND CONTEMPLATION AREA

The genteel life style of the scholar-official is revealed in many ways. Sumptuary laws provided him with an exclusive mode of dress and housing and his salary provided him with a corps of personal servants in addition to his wages of money and goods.[25] It is fitting then that his place of work should also be of a distinctive sort. The whole Imperial Library building complex was landscaped with meticulous care. Flagstone paths wound through a lush flora sustained by the semi-tropical climate of Hang-chou.[26]

North of the Compilation Hall cluster of buildings there was an area that was especially designed for rest and contemplation. In and about the area were pavilions where members of the staff took their tea.[27] An orange-tree grove surrounded by a stream of water could be seen from one of these pavilions. Beyond this there was a slope on which fifty or more pine and

fir trees grew along with wild tea amidst curious stones artfully arranged. Behind the slope there was an orchard with stands of plum and almond trees.[28]

SERVICE AREA

A building complex as large and as well landscaped as the one described above was in need of constant attention. Consequently, there were a number of service personnel on the grounds. For the most part they were located in space provided in lateral buildings on the inside of the south wall. Gardeners, carpenters, and others who kept up the Imperial Library building complex and its grounds had small places of their own. In addition, officials who mounted and dismounted their horses as they came and went from their offices were assisted by service personnel stationed in adjacent buildings.[29]

All in all, the location of the Library and its physical arrangements provided conveniences for the discharge of its functions, and at the same time fitted it to symbolize in its formal plan and attractive features the importance the state attached to all scholarly activity.

III. ADMINISTRATION AND PERSONNEL

The scholarly agencies were staffed with a well-organized corps of directive, operative, and service personnel. Each group performed a distinctive set of functions within the administrative structure. Moreover, responsibilities were clearly delineated for each agency and each member of the staff; however, higher level decisions often affected the staffing of the scholarly agencies, either accelerating the rate at which work was done or slowing it down. Regardless of these extra-agency concerns the administrative organization and personnel arrangements conformed to a basically consistent pattern.

Several aspects of the Imperial Library personnel administration lend it special interest. Among these are the governmental policy of directing much of its best new talent to directive positions in the Library, the place Library positions occupied in the future careers of these men, and the unusually full information we have on the careers of the lower bureaucrats and service personnel in this agency.

ADMINISTRATIVE HIERARCHY OF GOVERNMENT

The scholary agencies were units within the administrative hierarchy of the government, a hierarchy which had been established in the Northern Sung much as it had been in the T'ang.[1] The emperor was the head of state and sovereign in all matters. He gov-

---

[22] *NSKKL*(1) 2/7b–8a.

[23] *NSKKL*(1) 2/5b.

[24] *NSKKL*(1) 2/5a.

[25] See Appendix II, Imperial Library Wage Schedules and Personnel Data.

[26] See *NSKKL*(1) 2/1b–8a for details on landscaping.

[27] *NSKKL*(1) 2/5b.

[28] *NSKKL*(1) 2/6b–7b.

[29] *NSKKL*(1) 2/2a.

[1] Edward A. Kracke, Jr., *Civil Service in Early Sung China,* pp. 5–6.

erned the empire by means of a well-developed administrative apparatus which was directed by a small group of councilors of state. These councilors, serving as a cabinet to oversee affairs of state and to present measures to the emperor requiring his attention, were the heads of the three major departments into which the administrative structure of the government was organized. At first the Secretariat-Chancellery (*Chung-shu men-hsia*) executed policy in all areas except economic and military matters. Policies in these two areas were carried out by a Finance Commission (*San-ssu*) and a Bureau of Military Affairs (*Shu-mi yüan*).[2] In the reign of Emperor Shen Tsung this top structure was changed to comprise a Secretariat Department wherein government policy originated, a Chancellery Department which had the authority to review these policies and a Department of Ministries which was charged with the execution of approved policies. The Department of Ministries was divided into six ministries through which it directed the operation of numerous agencies. These agencies carried out a vast array of governmental functions.[3] There were several agencies, however, which were not under the control of any of the six ministries, but reported directly to the Department of Ministries.[4] Among these were the scholarly agencies (see fig. 1).

The most important scholarly agencies in the early Sung were the three institutes: the Chao Wen Institute, the Chi Hsien Library, and the Institute of History. In addition, there was an Imperial Archives which was subordinate to the three institutes.[5] These four agencies were housed in the Ch'ung Wen Library. Each of the three institutes and the Imperial Archives maintained a collection of writings, the use of which was supervised by the director (*Chien*) of the Ch'ung Wen Library. The writings under his supervision were the Imperial Library collections.[6] This loose organization appears to have resulted in a less than satisfactory level of control over the books. For instance, in 1059 an official memorialized to the effect that many items were missing from the collections because of the negligence of the director.[7] The situation was rectified in 1082 when the Imperial Library, much like its T'ang predecessor, was established in association with the other scholarly agencies. This agency assumed control of the collections in the Ch'ung Wen Library and supervised their use.

The re-organized Imperial Library directed the operation of four smaller agencies which dealt with the compilation of the calendar and related matters. These were the Office of the Calendar (*T'ai-shih chü*) which compiled and distributed the official calendar, the Bureau of Bells and Drums (*Chung-ku yüan*) which was responsible for ceremonial accouterments, the Clepsydra Office (*Ts'e-yen hun-i k'o-lou so*) which maintained a water clock and the Wen Te Hall (*Wen Te Tien*), apparently used for ceremonies.[8] As noted above, the Imperial Library was charged with the compilation of the "daily record" and the "selected documents." Its personnel carried out both of these tasks indirectly through the system of concurrent appointments. Members of its staff would concurrently hold the positions in the Daily Record Office and the Selected Documents Office.[9]

The other four scholarly agencies were related to the Department of Ministries in the same manner as the Imperial Library, that is, each one received its orders directly from it. Thus the five agencies were on a par with each other. Each of the four agencies had as its main function the compilation of the work indicated by its name. It should be noted, however, that the Imperial Library was the only one which was a continuously functioning agency. The other four operated only when there was a work to compile, and often it was the Imperial Library personnel who were assigned to the agency to do the job.

The internal organization of the scholarly agencies was simple and effective. As with other agencies of the government, work was organized around the "desk" (*an*). In the case of the Imperial Library there were four desks: a general services desk (*Chih-tsa an*) to handle personnel and related administrative matters, a library collections desk (*Ching-chi an*), a ceremonies desk (*Chu-pan an*), such as existed in all other major agencies, to prepare the Imperial Library to participate in ceremonies and a calendar desk (*T'ai-shih an*) to organize the work of the Office of the Calendar, the Bureau of Bells and Drums, the Clepsydra Office, and the Wen Te Hall.[10] The other scholarly agencies also organized their work around desks.[11]

IMPERIAL LIBRARY
DIRECTIVE PERSONNEL POSITIONS AND QUOTAS

The administrative reform of 1082 which brought the Imperial Library into being for the first time in

---

[2] *Ibid.*, pp. 28–32, 37–41.

[3] Edward A. Kracke, Jr., *Translation of Sung Civil Service Titles* (Paris, Sung Project, Ecole Pratique des Hautes Etudes, 1957), chart II, "The Sung Central Government after about 1080." The six ministries are the Ministry of Personnel (*Li-pu*), Ministry of Finance (*Hu-pu*), Ministry of Rites (*Li-pu*), Ministry of War (*Ping-pu*), Ministry of Justice (*Hsing-pu*), Ministry of Works (*Kung-pu*).

[4] *SHY:CK* 18/25a, 18/37a–37b.

[5] *LTKS* 1/3a; *SHY:CK* 18/2a.

[6] *LTKS* 1/2b. Note also the auxiliary official of the Chao Wen Institute (*Chih chao-wen kuan*) was in charge of collating, emending, copying, and compiling. It is not clear whether he did this for the three institutes or for the Chao Wen Institute alone. See *LTKS* 1/1b.

[7] *LTKS* 2/7a–7b.

[8] *SHY:CK* 18/25a, 18/31b; *NSKKL*(1) 10/2a–2b; Li Yu, *Sung-ch'ao shih-shih* (in: *Wu-ying tien chü-chen pan ch'üan-shu*, 1899), 9/19a–19b. Hereafter cited as *SCSS*.

[9] *SHY:CK* 18/37a, 18/37b; *TK* 51/16b; *SCSS* 9/16–19a; *NSKKL*(1) 4/8b–9a.

[10] *NSKKL*(1) 10/1a–2b.

[11] See for examples *NSKKL*(1) 2/5a.

TABLE 2

IMPERIAL LIBRARY DIRECTIVE PERSONNEL
POSITIONS AND QUOTAS

Position	Quotas			
	1082[a]	1131[b]	1134[c]	1135[d]
Director of the Imperial Library	1	1[e]	1[f]	—
Vice-director of the Imperial Library	1	—	—	—
Executive assistant of the Imperial Library	1	1	1	—
Staff author	1	1	2	2
Librarian of the Imperial Library	2	—	1	2
Assistant staff author	2	1	2	2
Collator of the Imperial Library	4	2	4	12[g]
Correcting editor of the Imperial Library	2	2	4	—
Total	14[h]	8	15	18

[a] *SHY:CK* 18/2a–2b; 18/21a. Dated 1082, 5th month.

[b] *SHY:CK* 18/24b; *SCSS* 9/14b; T'o T'o and others, *Sung shih*, 117/7b. Dated 1131, 2d month, 19th day. Hereafter cited as *SS*.

[c] This is a revision of the 1131, 2d month, 19th day quota. *SHY:CK* 18/26b. Dated 1134, 6th month, 18th day, and 1134, 4th month, 16th day.

[d] *SHY:CK* 18/26b; *YH* 121/51b–52a; *SCSS* 9/15a; *SS* 117/9b. Dated 1135, 8th month, 3rd day. There is another source, *SHY:CK* 18/1b, which gives the same quota, but dated 1145. It appears to be a copyist error. No other quota dated 1145 has come to light and the Institute of History mentioned in the passage was abolished in 1140.

[e] Or one vice-director of the Imperial Library.

[f] Or one vice-director of the Imperial Library.

[g] A total of twelve collators and correcting editors of the Imperial Library.

[h] The number of directive personnel actually assigned was perhaps eight. See *SHY:CK* 18/3a.

the Sung as a separate agency of government also provided for a well-integrated staff consisting of three groups: directive, operative, and service personnel. The directive personnel functioned as the executive members of the staff. These men were in the civil service. The operative personnel were professional assistants to the directive personnel. Whereas the latter seldom served more than two years in the Imperial Library before being re-assigned, the operative personnel were provided with a pattern of promotion which gave them a career in the Imperial Library extending over an adult's working years. These men appear to have been responsible for carrying out the daily operation of the Imperial Library. The last group consisted of service personnel. These men carried out many tasks ancillary to the operation of the Imperial Library, but nonetheless necessary to make it perform well.

The 1082 directive personnel slate included eight positions with a separate quota for each one. Combined they totaled fourteen members. Although the quota for each position changed in subsequent years,

the slate remained the same throughout the remainder of the Sung. On occasion additional positions were created, but for specific purposes and for limited periods of time only (see table 2).

As originally established in 1082 the directive personnel slate consisted of a director of the Imperial Library, assisted by a vice-director of the Imperial Library and an executive assistant of the Imperial Library. These three officials supervised the operation of this agency. A staff author and two assistant staff authors compiled the "daily record," the "selected documents," and provided liturgies for sacrificial ceremonies.[12] Two librarians of the Imperial Library cared for the collections. The four collators of the Imperial Library and two correcting editors of the Imperial Library bore the responsibility for the accuracy of the texts in the collections.[13] Although they did not do all of the collating and emending, those who held these two positions did supervise the copying and subsequent checking of each text as executed by the operative personnel.

These are the designated functions of the directive personnel; however, in the tradition of the Chinese civil service, duties were flexible and men were expected to perform a variety of tasks in addition to those of the position to which they were assigned. Thus in the absence of the staff author or the assistant staff authors, their functions could be carried out by a collator or correcting editor of the Imperial Library, but only temporarily.[14] Quite often directive personnel were given concurrent appointments in one of the scholarly agencies, in this manner adding functions outside the range of their designated duties. For the staff author and assistant staff authors mentioned above, this was the normal procedure.[15]

With the exception of the director and vice-director, Imperial Library directive personnel positions were of a rather low rank in the superior civil service. In the nine-grade scheme, in which each grade was subdivided once, six of the eight directive positions ranked in the bottom third of the scheme and only the director and vice-director were in the second third. None were in the top third. As the total monthly wage and per-

---

[12] The compilation of the "daily record" was the exclusive preserve of the men who occupied these two positions. In carrying out the compilation of this work they were not to be interfered with by their superiors, that is, the director, vice-director, and executive assistant of the Imperial Library. See *SHY:CK* 18/6a.

[13] The men who filled the two positions of collator and correcting editor of the Imperial Library were examined (*chao-shih*) at the Bureau of Academicians (*Hsüeh-shih yüan*) prior to appointment. The examination is more clearly described in the Northern Sung, but apparently was used in the Southern Sung. See *Sung hui-yao chi-kao* (Taipei, 1967), *hsüan-chü* 31/12a–23b on the *chao-shih*. Hereafter cited as *SHY:HC* 18/1b, 18/3a, 18/7a on the form of this examination.

[14] *SHY:CK* 18/6b.

[15] See *NSKKL*(1) 8/9a–14a for examples.

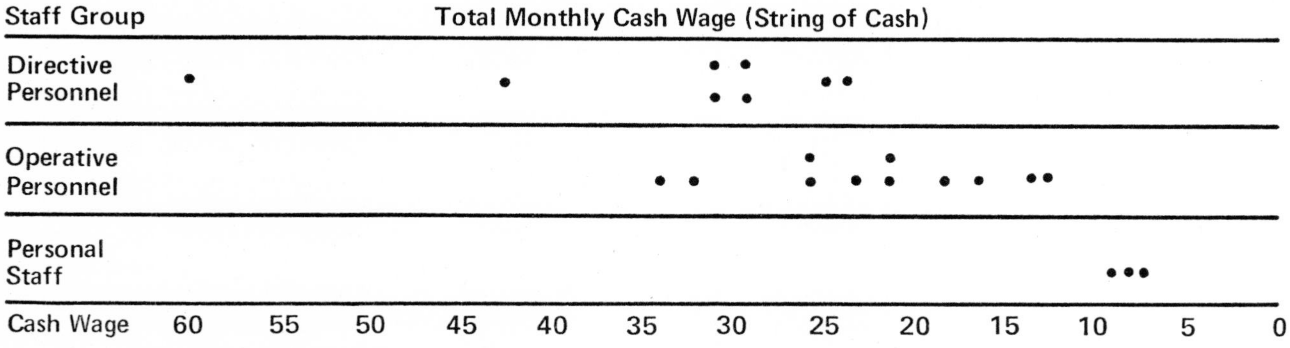

Staff Group	Total Monthly Cash Wage (String of Cash)												

Directive Personnel	•	•	• • / • •	• •
Operative Personnel	• •	• / • / • • • / • • / • •
Personal Staff	• • •

| Cash Wage | 60 | 55 | 50 | 45 | 40 | 35 | 30 | 25 | 20 | 15 | 10 | 5 | 0 |

Fig. 5. Relative table of wage schedules. See appendix II, tables 8, 9, 10 for complete wage schedules.

sonal staff for the slate indicates, there was a significant difference in the standing of the second third and the bottom third in the superior service. As with the administrative organization, the directive personnel staff was reactivated in the Southern Sung largely as it had been established in 1082.

IMPERIAL LIBRARY
DIRECTIVE PERSONNEL QUOTAS AND APPOINTMENTS, 1131–1190

A temporary slate of six Imperial Library directive personnel positions with a combined quota of eight persons was established in 1131. Either a director or a vice-director of the Imperial Library was to be appointed, but not both, and no provision was made for a librarian of the Imperial Library. In the middle of 1134 the position of librarian was created. This increased the number of positions to be filled at one time to seven. The combined quota for these seven positions, however, was raised to fifteen, almost twice the figure for the temporary quota. Another adjustment in directive personnel positions and quotas was made a year later, in 1135, the final adjustment in the period 1131–1190. It provided for five positions in addition to a director or vice-director, and an executive assistant of the Imperial Library. The combined quota for those five positions was eighteen persons. Including the director or vice-director and executive assistant of the Imperial Library, however, there were seven positions to be filled at one time, giving a total for all positions of twenty persons.

Actual appointments of directive personnel to the Imperial Library fell short of the combined quotas for all positions throughout the period 1131–1190, but often they did equal and on occasion exceeded the numbers designated for certain positions.[16] The skele-

---

[16] This slate of Imperial Library personnel was modeled after an earlier T'ang quota. Prior to 738 there were four staff authors, four librarians, eight collators, and two correcting editors of the Imperial Library, for a total of eighteen exclusive of the supervisory members of the staff. See Wang P'u, *T'ang hui-yao* (in: *Wu-ying tien chü-chen pan ch'üan-shu*, 1899), 65/1b–2a.

ton staff maintained in the Imperial Library in the years 1131 to 1133 and the consequent minimal level of its activities beyond acquisition reflect the uncertainty of governmental operations resulting from the persistent attacks of the Jurchen armies (see figs. 5 and 6).

For the decade which followed (1134–1143), while the Imperial Library was located in Hang-chou at the Fa Hui Temple, the staff was kept to nearly full quota capacity. Apparently it was in this decade that a concerted effort was made to prepare the texts which had been collected for use. The effort to gather works continued also, but at a milder pace after 1135.

In 1143, the year in which construction began on the new Imperial Library quarters, the number of directive personnel appointments started to fall off. By the next year, after the building complex was completed, the staff was down to one-half of full complement and in 1146 to one-fourth, which was the high through the year 1154. With the collections basically reconstituted and prepared for use again after 1143 and no scholarly projects under way, there was little need for anything more than a skeleton staff. In the year 1155 the number of directive personnel on the staff began to rise once more. It reached four-fifths of capacity in 1158, only to slip to two-fifths in 1161. This rise and fall is coincidental with the compilation of the *San-ch'ao kuo-shih,* reign histories for three Northern Sung administrations.[17]   During the six

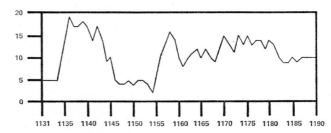

Fig. 6. Fluctuation in directive personnel appointments, 1131–1190. Data drawn from table 13.

[17] *NSKKL* (1) 4/6b; *SHY:CK* 18/53b.

years which followed, the staff remained slightly above one-half of full complement only to slip slightly again in 1168. From 1169 through 1181 the range was between one-half and three-quarters capacity. Thereafter the number of directive personnel remained at slightly less than one-half of the combined quota for all positions.

The constant fluctuation in directive personnel appointments after 1143 appears to have been more in response to the extent to which official histories were being compiled rather than the special needs of the Imperial Library, except for the years 1177 and 1178. In the latter two years its operations were summed up for the first time in the Southern Sung with the publication of the *Nan Sung kuan-ko lu*, a compilation of material on the Southern Sung Imperial Library and associated scholarly agencies, and the first Southern Sung Imperial Library catalog (*Chung-hsing kuan-ko shu-mu*).

The rise and fall in the number of directive personnel on duty in the Imperial Library exemplifies the flexibility in personnel assignment in the Sung civil service and the degree to which work was being carried on in this agency. In accordance with specific needs directive personnel were appointed to the staff, but not beyond the combined total of quotas which evidently was a maximum complement of personnel.

The combined quota of two for the three highest positions on the directive personnel slate, director or vice-director and executive assistant of the Imperial Library, was filled to full capacity through 1140. For the next two years their numbers declined to one-half. It rose to full capacity in 1143 and 1144, a point not reached again until 1155. From 1155 to 1190 these positions were filled in accordance with the quotas except for 1172, 1182, and 1189, at which times only an executive assistant was on duty and in 1175 and 1178 when the quotas were oversubscribed. The year 1175 is significant in that it is the first of nine years in which a director was appointed. Normally a vice-director was in charge, but in several cases an executive assistant directed its operations. These three positions then, comprising the supervisory team of the Imperial Library, were generally filled as designated by the quotas regardless of the level of Imperial Library activity.

Staff authors and assistant staff authors were absent from the staff for the years 1131 and 1132; thereafter, at least one man was appointed to one of the two positions. Only once, in 1145, was the full complement assigned. These positions remained staffed at one-half of the quota or less from 1145 to 1169. Throughout the 1170's and 1180's they were filled to three-fourths of capacity, with the exception of 1185 when they were half filled. This suggests a moderately sustained effort at compiling official history, a function of the Imperial Library, and one which was carried on at its own pace apart from the bibliographic work of the agency.

The position of librarian was filled to quota capacity through 1143. For the twenty-six-year period from 1144 to 1169 it was vacant almost three-fourths of the time, suggesting an interest in the collections less intense than in the period 1131 to 1143. In the last two decades of the period under discussion, that is 1170 to 1190, this quota was filled as designated, with two cases of over-staffing and two of under-staffing, demonstrating a revival of interest in the holdings which persisted until 1190.

Appointments to the positions of collator and correcting editor of the Imperial Library became significant in the year 1135 at which time ten men were appointed. For the next seven years, while the collections were being prepared for use, the quota was filled to between three-fourths and full capacity. In 1143 it slipped to almost one-half of capacity, in 1144 and 1145 to one-third and through 1155 to one-fourth or less. From 1156 to 1181 it ranged rather freely between slightly less than one-half and three-fourths. Thereafter it reached a high of one-third of full capacity, but then only once. For the most part during the last decade of the period under discussion the quota was filled to one-quarter of capacity or less. Again, after the initial effort to prepare the holdings for use came to an end in 1143, there was little need for the full quota of these staff members. Moreover, those who were appointed spent at least part of their time on scholarly projects.

IMPERIAL LIBRARY
DIRECTIVE PERSONNEL AS AN ELITE GROUP WITHIN THE CIVIL SERVICE

In the tradition of the Chinese civil service, each man served in a variety of positions and few if any spent their entire careers in one area of governmental activity.[18] This is borne out by a study of pertinent aspects of the careers of the 315 men who probably constituted the total number who served in the Imperial Library from 1131 to 1190. If an official could not make a career as a scholar-librarian then what was the significance of an appointment to the Imperial Library for superior service personnel? The data suggest that they were chosen from among the most promising members of the service to be judged for promotion to positions of greater responsibility in the government.[19]

It has been tentatively estimated that 56 per cent to 63 per cent of the replacements required for the upper service during the period 1142 to 1171 entered by

---

[18] Edward A. Kracke, Jr., *Civil Service in Early Sung China*, pp. 87–90.

[19] See Edward A. Kracke, Jr., *Civil Service in Early Sung China*, p. 223 for a comment by a contemporary of Wang An-shih on the desirability of assignment to the scholarly agencies.

means other than the triennial upper civil service examination (*chin-shih*). Those data are not conclusive, but perhaps no more than one-half entered by way of this examination which was considered a prerequisite for "advancement to the more important governmental positions." [20] Of the 315 persons who had served in the Imperial Library from 1131 to 1190, 95.8 per cent or 302 had passed the upper service examination. The remainder were given a special examination prior to appointment and if passed granted the status of one who had successfully passed the civil service examination. [21]

That Imperial Library appointees were an elite even among those who passed the civil service examination is further suggested by the fact that all examination laureates (*Chuang-yüan*), that is men who placed first from the years 1132 to 1190, served as directive personnel (see table 12). This is further confirmed by a study of the standing of the personnel on the civil service examinations. It suggests that they were required to have passed high on the list.

In regular examination practice all successful examinees were placed in order of their marks. The list was then divided into five groups (*chia*) and regrouped as follows: those in group one and two were designated "passed with distinction" (*chi-ti*); group three, "formally qualified" (*ch'u-shen*) and group four and five, "passed" (*t'ung-ch'u-shen*). [22] Using the two extant Southern Sung upper service examination lists dated 1148 and 1256 as a datum, we find that proportionally the number in corresponding groups in the two lists were very similar. Fewer men were assigned to the first group than to the second, to the second than to the third, to the third than to the fourth, and to the fourth than to the fifth. The greatest difference in number occurs between groups three and four. [23]

The first three groups, those who "passed with distinction" and those who "formally qualified," constitute 20 per cent of the total in the 1148 list and 23.3 per cent in the 1256 list, yet of Imperial Library appointees who passed the examinations, 78.8 per cent placed in these first three groups. Not only was it virtually a necessity to have passed the superior civil service examination for appointment to the Imperial Library, but a standing in the upper quarter of the list was almost mandatory.

Confirmation of this and a final indication that Imperial Library appointees were an elite group is to be found in the percentage of chief councilors of state (*Tsai-hsiang*) and assisting councilors (*Chih-cheng*) who had served during their careers in the Imperial Library. Of the twenty-three chief councilors and ninety-nine assisting councilors who served between 1131 and 1190, 30.4 per cent of the former and 30.3 per cent of the latter had previously served in the Imperial Library. [24] When compared with the figure of only 4.2 per cent of the persons on the 1148 examination list who at any time served in the Imperial Library, it is an indication of the frequency of service in the Imperial Library among those who rose high in the government.

TENURE OF OFFICE AND CONTINUITY OF POLICY IMPLEMENTATION

Characteristically, these men in the various directive positions remained on duty in the Imperial Library less than two years before transfer. The average service for the 290 directive personnel for whom we have civil service examination data (out of 302 in all) is 25.3 months, with 53.1 per cent serving for less than one year and 82.7 per cent serving for less than two years. Superior civil service examination laureates on the average served 33.6 months, 8.3 months above average. Given their special status the longer tour of duty is understandable. The average service periods for future chief councilors and assisting councilors, however, was 21.6 months and 20.6 months, respectively. No doubt their superiors recognized them as men of executive talent and quickly moved them on to service in other governmental agencies where needs were more pressing. Moreover, of the 290, only 14.5 per cent returned to the Imperial Library after their initial appointment. These two factors would appear to have impaired the consistent implementation of policy in the Imperial Library (see tables 14 and 15).

Fortunately, there were things which tended to mitigate this potential disruption of its operation. It was a rather small administrative unit and confined to one location. This enabled responsible parties to contact each other easily and facilitate operations. Further-

---

[20] Edward A. Kracke, Jr., "Family vs. Merit in Chinese Civil Service Examinations under the Empire," *Harvard Jour. Asiatic Studies* **10** (1947): p. 121. Except for a limited number of special cases all persons who entered the civil service by means of examination in the period 1131–1190 took it in "letters" (*chin-shih*). See *TK* 32/32b–34a. Hence the term "civil service examination" alone is used.

[21] In the period 1131–1190 twelve persons assigned to the Imperial Library were designated *t'zu chin-shih* and one *t'e-t'zu chin-shih*. These are distinct from the 302 *chin-shih*. The twelve *t'zu chin-shih* were already in the civil service, but they had entered by means other than the civil service examination. Thus it appears that they were granted *t'zu chin-shih* status in order that they might serve in the Imperial Library. See *SHY:HC* 9/1a–20a for examples of this procedure. Undoubtedly the single *t'e-t'zu chin-shih* is another case of a person being granted the status of *chin-shih* in order that he might serve in the Imperial Library.

[22] Edward A. Kracke, Jr., *Civil Service in Early Sung China*, pp. 66–67.

[23] An exception occurs in the 1256 list where fewer men appear in group five than in group four, but still the significant division is between three and four. See Appendix II, table 11

for the full set of figures of successful examinees in the years 1148 and 1256.

[24] *SS* 213/6a–28a.

more, the limited period of tenure for Imperial Library personnel was partly compensated by the maturity of most officials given such appointments. The average span of time from civil service examination date to initial appointment in the Imperial Library for the group of 290 directive personnel under consideration was 18.9 years.[25] Thus a man would normally be at least midway in his career upon appointment, and well experienced in government. As men were appointed to the Imperial Library to be assessed for promotion to positions of greater responsibility in government, however, examination laureates who entered the civil service with the most promise of high achievement, were appointed to the Imperial Library on an average of 3.1 years after their examinations. Two groups without such distinction but of obvious ability, those ultimately destined to be chief councilors and assisting councilors, were also appointed to the Imperial Library well before the average length of prior service. In the case of future chief councilors, 9.1 years elapsed between civil service examination date and appointment to the Imperial Library and in that of assisting councilors, 12.1 years. Thus, examination laureates who had entered the service with special distinction, could expect Imperial Library appointments with only brief experience in government, while those not so distinguished but of obvious ability, evidencing in their early careers the signs of future distinction, could enter such service after only a decade or so of experience. For the most part, however, some two decades would elapse before a man could expect to serve in the Imperial Library.

Although 85.5 per cent of the directive personnel who served once in the Imperial Library would not serve again, those who did so returned to positions of greater responsibility. Moreover, those who entered with no experience usually served in the two lowest positions, that is collator and correcting editor of the Imperial Library, before assuming more responsible duties. For instance, there is a rather close correlation between position and experience among directors, vice-directors, and executive assistants who served previously in the Imperial Library. Whereas all the directors of the Imperial Library and one-half of the vice-directors had served previously, only 15 per cent of the executive assistants had had such experience. Former service was valued in the positions of staff author and assistant staff author, as 85 per cent of the former and 78 per cent of the latter had served previously. This is in contrast to the low figure of 36 per cent of the librarians who had Imperial Library experience upon appointment. No doubt in the case of the staff author and assistant staff author the responsibilities of document compilation and history writing required experience. Although former service was less frequent among librarians it was probably not so

necessary, since the collections were largely reconstituted and ready for use after 1143, and their duties were more routine. More experience would be needed by staff authors and assistant staff authors who were more or less continually involved in the compiling and writing. The operative personnel, to be discussed next, must have also provided a measure of continuity to Imperial Library operations, thus mitigating the effect of directive personnel mobility.

OPERATIVE PERSONNEL

Operative personnel assisted in the management of the Imperial Library and in the accomplishment of scholarly tasks. It appears to have been a stable group and as such capable of aiding in the consistent implementation of policy and practice. Their system of recruitment and promotion was organized so as to provide a career throughout the adult years for those selected to serve.

The recruitment and promotion of operative personnel proceeded in accordance with a well-defined system of regulations. It was not permissible to have been an itinerant laborer or a person of questionable character. These qualifications had to be attested to by three operative personnel staff members who held the billet of senior copyist and above [26] (see tables 3 and 9).

The difficulty of entering into the operative personnel career was increased by a recruitment examination in reading and writing administered by the directive personnel on duty in the Imperial Library. Later in the Northern Sung, candidates were required both to read and write 300 characters from the *Meng-tzu* without making ten errors in either part of the examination.[27] Those admitted to the corps were reexamined after a one-year probationary period. This time they had to read 300 characters from the *Mao* version of the *Book of Poetry* and 300 from the *Lao-tzu* without making ten mistakes in either text, plus write an official document (*cha*) free from error.[28] In the Southern Sung the recruitment examinations for operative personnel seem to have been the same. Our data are limited, but what remains agrees with the system outlined above. It was still necessary to write 300 characters from the *Book of Poetry* and 300 characters from the *Meng-tzu* with less than ten errors in each text and to demonstrate an ability to read.[29]

Having passed the recruitment examination, new staff members were assigned to the lowest billet on the operative personnel slate, that of apprentice. Judg-

---

[25] *SS* 213/6a–28a.

[26] *LTKS Pu*/7a; *NSKKL*(1) 10/4a.
[27] The character '*shu*' in *NSKKL*(1) 10/4a has been read "to write," rather than the "Book of History." This appears to be in keeping with the text in *LTKS Pu*/7a. Apparently the operative personnel actually copied a text, rather than wrote it from memory or in the case of the official document, actually composed it.
[28] *LTKS Pu*/7a.
[29] *NSKKL*(1) 10/4a.

ing from the examination scheme of the late Northern Sung, appointments were temporary until the second examination was passed. There was no limit to the number who could be appointed to this billet, but it does not appear to have been large as appointments were made when vacancies appeared in the billet of corrector which was immediately above.[30]

Thus newly appointed apprentices apparently took the place of those who succeeded in passing the examination which qualified them for the billet of corrector. Having already demonstrated an ability to read and write on two occasions, candidates for this billet were given the simpler task of writing a passage from the *Book of Rites* (*Chou i*) or the *Book of Filial Piety* (*Hsiao ching*). It was necessary to pass the same examination for promotion to copyist.[31]

From senior copyist to director of operative personnel, promotion was based largely on seniority. Each billet in the slate represented a step for these men, and operative personnel spent one and one-half years in each one.[32] There were twelve steps in the adjusted slate of operative personnel for 1133 which would have required nineteen and one-half years to complete. The final step was promotion to Classification Title 40 (CT40), the lowest in a ranking scheme for directive personnel,[33] for which operative personnel were eligible upon completion of a one and one-half year term as director of operative personnel or twenty-five years of service.[34]

Promotion from step to step was not automatic. One had to be a member in good standing. For instance, a criminal offense could lead to a one and one-half year term being eliminated from the culprit's service records, thus prolonging the length of time before he was eligible for Classification Title 40.[35]

This intricate organization of operative personnel appears to have been devised to provide an able corps of assistants for the directive personnel. The character reference qualification no doubt was designed to recruit reliable men, whereas the reading and writing examinations were given to insure a level of literacy necessary to carry out the tasks assigned. The step-by-step promotion scheme guaranteed the able and interested staff members directive personnel status late in adult life, a standing of no mean proportions in Sung China. Such an arrangement no doubt made for stability among the operative personnel which in turn added a

---

[30] *NSKKL*(1) 10/4a.

[31] *NSKKL*(1) 10/4a.

[32] *NSKKL*(1) 10/1a–1b. Apparently no examination was required for promotion from *Shou-ch'üeh* to *Tu-k'ung mu-kuan* and there is no indication of the criteria for promotion from *Cheng-hsi-ming* to *Shou-ch'üeh* and *Shou ch'üeh* to *Cheng-ming k'ai-shu*.

[33] Edward A. Kracke, Jr., *Translation of Sung Civil Service Titles*, pp. 4 and 10.

[34] *NSKKL*(1) 10/4a.

[35] *NSKKL*(1) 10/4b.

TABLE 3

OPERATIVE PERSONNEL BILLETS, QUOTAS, AND WAGES

Billet	Translation[a]	Quota[b] 1133	Monthly[c] cash wage
Tu-k'ung-mu kuan	Director of Operative Personnel	1	33.50
K'ung-mu kuan	Vice-director of Operative Personnel	1	31.50
Ssu-k'u shu-chih kuan	Assistant writer in the Four Collections	1	25.50
Shu-chih kuan	Assistant writer	1	25.50
Piao-tsou kuan	Palace courier	1	22.50
Shu-k'u kuan	Library attendant	1	20.50
Shou-tang kuan	Chief of copyists	2	20.50
Cheng-ming k'ai-shu	Senior copyist	5	17.45
Shou-ch'üeh	Senior corrector	1	15.95
Cheng-hsi-ming	Copyist	5	13.45
Shou-ch'üeh hsi-ming	Corrector	5	12.45
T'ou-ming-jen	Apprentice	No limit	—

[a] While we know the general function of the operative personnel as a group and something of the procedures for their recruitment and promotion as well as their relative standing, number, and pay, our knowledge of their specific functions is almost wholly limited to what might be implied from the literal meaning of their titles. The *Tu-k'ung-mu kuan* (also titled *Tien-chien wen-tzu*), assisted by the *K'ung-mu kuan*, apparently headed the staff. Robert des Rotours, without mentioning the former, considers the latter to be a "fonctionnaire charge des services administratifs." See des Rotours, *Histoire de Ngan Lou-chan*, pp. 362–363. Perhaps in T'ang times the position of *Tu-k'ung-mu kuan* did not exist. Yet, it is clear from a literal translation of his title, his standing on the list, and pay, that he was the superior of *K'ung-mu kuan*. Thus we suggest that the *Tu-k'ung-mu kuan* be considered the director of operative personnel and the *K'ung-mu kuan*, vice-director of operative personnel. Below the vice-director was the *Ssu k'u shu-chih kuan* and the *Shu-chih kuan* who appear to be assistant writers. See des Rotours, *Traité des Fonctionnaires* 1: p. 194; 2: p. 585. The *Piao-tsou kuan* might be the palace courier. See des Rotours, *Traité des Fonctionnaires* 2: p. 567. Next in rank stood the *Shu-k'u kuan* who is probably the library attendant. The title *Shou-tang kuan* is perhaps chief of copyists. Other agencies of government also had this operative personnel billet. Next is the *Cheng-ming k'ai-shu*. Judging from des Rotours, *Traité des Fonctionnaires* 1: p. 173 and *YH* 165/27b he is a copyist. Perhaps he was assisted by the *Shou-ch'üeh*. Below this is the *Cheng hsi-ming*, and the *Shou-ch'üeh hsi-ming* who appear to have been copyists also. See *NSKKL*(1) 10/3b. The *T'ou-ming-jen*, an apprentice, completed the list.

[b] Originally, 1131, 4th month, 14th day, a temporary quota of two *Shu-k'u kuan* and ten *Cheng-ming k'ai-shu* had been established. See *NSKKL*(1) 10/3a. On 1133, 5th month, 15th day another quota was established. See *NSKKL*(1) 10/3a; *SHY:CK* 18/26a. This was modified in only one respect. The number of *Cheng-ming k'ai-shu* was raised from three to five on 1133, 6th month, 19th day. See *NSKKL*(1) 10/3a; *SHY:CK* 18/26b. Note also, in 1133, 5th month, 13th day list in *NSKKL*(1) 10/3a the *Shu-chih kuan* is omitted. This quota of 1133, 6th month, 10th day remained the same through 1190, except for an occasional change in the number of *Cheng-hsi-ming* and *Shou-ch'üeh hsi-ming*. See *NSKKL*(1) 10/3a–3b.

[c] Figures are for strings of cash. For an explanation of this term see table 4, note b. See also appendix II, table 9 for the full operative personnel wage schedule.

TABLE 4

IMPERIAL LIBRARY DIRECTIVE PERSONNEL
RANKS AND WAGES

Position	Rank[a]	Monthly[b] cash wage	Personal[c] staff
Director of the Imperial Library	4a	60	10
Vice-director of the Imperial Library	5b	42	7
Executive assistant of the Imperial Library	7b	31	3
Staff author	7b	31	3
Librarian of the Imperial Library	8a	29	3
Assistant staff author	8a	29	3
Collator of the Imperial Library	8b	25	2
Correcting editor of the Imperial Library	8b	24	2

[a] The same ranks are given in *SHY:CK* 18/1a–1b and 18/2a–2b. They are dated to the reign of Emperor Shen Tsung and the beginning of the reign period (1131–1163), respectively.

[b] Figures indicate strings of cash (*kuan*). A string of cash, that is a string of round coins, was the money of account in Sung China. It was valued at 1,000 cash but actually contained only 770 copper coins. These coins, strung together in units of 77 and valued at 100, circulated in the empire. Whenever it was necessary to express a financial transaction, it was done in terms of the number of strings of cash or a fraction thereof. Hence, each of the sixty strings of cash received monthly by the Director of the Imperial Library actually contained only 770 coins. The purchasing power of this and other salaries is not known.

[c] For the full wage schedule see Appendix II, Table 10.

measure of excellence and continuity to the implementation of Imperial Library policies and practices.

SERVICE PERSONNEL

In addition to directive and operative personnel, the Imperial Library was staffed with a host of service personnel. These included gate attendants, who were under the direction of a military officer, firemen, cooks, binders, and messengers.[36] We are not well informed on the working conditions or career potential of these members of the staff. Yet the services they performed were essential if the Imperial Library were to run well (see table 10).

The relative standing of these three segments of the Imperial Library staff is roughly indicated by the total monthly cash wage each received. A director of the Imperial Library received a total monthly cash wage well above the vice-director and he somewhat more than the remainder of the directive personnel. Significantly the wages of those on the top half of the operative personnel slate are comparable to the remaining three-fourths of the directive personnel slate. Thus, total monthly wages suggest that the operative personnel corps was only of a slightly lower standing than the directive personnel. The personal staff of the directive personnel, which might be taken as a rough equivalent of the service personnel segment of the Imperial Library staff, stood well below these

[36] *NSKKL* (1) 10/5a–5b.

other two groups of personnel which almost form a continuum judging from total monthly cash wages (see table 4).

Thus the personnel policies of the Imperial Library served several quite different purposes. In the directive group the middle-aged officials who had passed the difficult superior examinations moderately well were supplemented by a smaller number of younger colleagues who had demonstrated special brilliance, and also—at least in the lower directive ranks—by those who had risen from the operative corps through prolonged good service. Morale was no doubt encouraged among the lower bureaucrats by hope of rise, thus an element of creative brilliance must have been introduced above, and an added element of scholarly experience, valued in the political thought of the time, was introduced among the empire's policy makers.

IV. SCHOLARSHIP AND BOOKS

The major activity of the scholarly agencies was document compilation and history writing. Sizable quantities of material were produced and in part made available to the scholarly community. It was the Imperial Library which produced the "daily record," the document on which the works compiled and written by the scholarly agencies was based. In addition, the Imperial Library maintained the largest collection of books and documents in government and society. Its collections served the needs of the government in the conduct of official business, including the work of the scholarly agencies, and to a limited degree the scholarly community outside of the government.

DOCUMENT COMPILATION AND HISTORY WRITING

The scholarly agencies generated a number of significant works in the Southern Sung. At various times these agencies edited the ancient writings that constituted the canon of orthodox belief, compiled encyclopedias, collected the writings of individuals, and wrote histories.[1] These projects were carried out for the benefit of the emperor, the government, the scholarly community, and in several instances for the literate populace at large. Yet the core activity of these agencies and their reason for existence remained document compilation and history writing. They drew on three principal sources for their material: the accounts of imperial activity in government, the records of ministerial meetings[2] and documents in the archives of

[1] Chu Hsi relates an instance of the Reign Chronicle Bureau engaging in scholarly activity outside the realm of document compilation and history writing. See Chu Hsi, *Hui-an hsien-sheng Chu-wen kung wen-chi* (*SPTK*), 21/27b–28a. Hereafter cited as *CHWC*. Another instance is reported in Chou Pi-ta, *Yü-t'ang lei-hui* (in: *Chou-i kuo-wen chung-kung chi*), 17/2b.

[2] The *shih-cheng chi* retained this name until 1171. After that time it was called the *hsüan-lun sheng-yü*. See NSKKL

governmental agencies.[3] The first was compiled by specially appointed recording officials, and the second by the councillors of state. None of these source materials were prepared in the scholarly agencies.[4]

On the basis of these materials the scholarly agencies prepared the "daily record," a detailed chronological account of governmental affairs prepared for each reign after it ended. It was done by the Daily Record Office which was manned by the staff author and assistant staff authors who were officials in the Imperial Library, the agency which ultimately was charged with the compilation of this work. More or less simultaneously another kind of work was being compiled by another scholarly agency with the same type of administrative apparatus. This was the "selected documents," a work arranged topically according to the organization of government and chronologically under each agency. As with the first work described above, the Imperial Library staff author and assistant staff authors were assigned to the Selected Documents Office to compile the "selected documents" for an earlier reign, but usually for the one just ended. Again the Imperial Library ultimately was repsonsible for the compilation of this type of work.

The "selected documents" were essentially manuals to assist officials in the conduct of governmental affairs. An official assigned to a new office might find himself in a totally new area of activity. In the conduct of business he could readily consult the "selected documents" for precedents.[5] This stood in contrast to the "daily record" which served essentially as the basic source for the two types of histories written by the two remaining scholarly agencies. These were the "reign chronicles" and the "reign histories" compiled by the Reign Chronicle Bureau and the Reign History Bureau respectively. The reign chronicles, in the tradition of the *Spring and Autumn Annals,* were accounts of each reign compiled in a successor reign. The reign histories, in the tradition of Ssu-ma Ch'ien's *Historical Records,* were cast in three parts: imperial annals (*ti-chi*), biographies (*lieh-chuan*) and monographs (*chih*). These, too, were compiled by successor reigns with the added characteristic of being prepared in editions of two or more reigns on occasion, perhaps subliminally in anticipation of the standard history which would be written for the whole dynasty by its successor.[6]

RECONSTITUTION OF THE IMPERIAL LIBRARY COLLECTIONS

The work of the scholarly agencies was largely dependent on the existence of the Imperial Library, both because it compiled the work which was basic to the whole process of history writing, the "daily record," and because it provided the library collections to support the compilation and writing activities. As noted above, however, the whole Imperial Library collection was lost to the Jurchen invaders in 1127. Consequently, it was necessary to reconstitute them anew south of the Yangtze River.

The reconstitution of the Imperial Library collections began almost immediately after it was reactivated in 1131. Large contributions of significant works were made through the year 1135, but from 1136 to 1143 there is less evidence that works were acquired by the Imperial Library or that its staff even sought items. This latter period appears to have been a time for consolidation, a time when the works collected in the years 1131 to 1135 were prepared for use.

As noted above, the number of directive personnel on the staff of the Imperial Library reflected this change in the pace of activity. In the beginning of the period of intense acquisition there were only five members on the staff, but by the end there were fifteen. Throughout the period of consolidation the staff remained at fourteen to nineteen members, all of whom appear to have busied themselves preparing the recently acquired texts for use. Almost no mention is made of acquisitions in this period.

The year 1143 appeared to be an auspicious one for the Imperial Library. Construction began on its permanent quarters and a proclamation was issued to search out more writings for the collection.[7] In 1144 the new buildings were completed and to guide the acquisition effort an intendent of the Imperial Library was appointed.[8] The new quarters were successfully

---

(1) 4/10a; *Sung hui-yao chi-kao* (Taipei, 1967), *yün-li* 1/28a. Hereafter cited as *SHY:YL.*

[3] *SHY:YL* 1/15b; *YH* 46/46a–46b.

[4] Apparently officials traveled to units of local government on occasion to gather material which would become part of the 'daily record.' See Liu Cheng, *Huang Sung Chung-hsing liang ch'ao sheng-cheng* Taipei, 1968), 9/13b–14a. Hereafter cited as *CHSC.*

[5] *NSKKL*(2) 4/4b.

[6] *NSKKL*(2) 4/1b. The order of compilation and writing presented in this section is based on a detailed study of the dates the scholarly projects were initiated and completed. In the process of collecting these data it became evident that other types of works were compiled by the scholarly agencies, but on a sporadic basis. Prominent among these were the *pao-hsün* and the *sheng-cheng* which were collections of imperial documents. The purpose of this whole process of document compilation and history writing was to provide a record of each reign. The tendency was to compile more types of works for each reign, hence the compilation of the *pao-hsün* and the *sheng-cheng*. These were not compiled for each reign, but this is the framework which guided those which were compiled.

[7] *NSKKL*(1) 3/1b.

[8] The intendant of the Imperial Library was one of the occasional special appointees to the directive personnel staff. The special assignment of this official was to search for writings formerly in the Northern Sung Imperial Library collections for its counterpart in the Southern Sung. This position was established for the first time after the administrative reform of the Imperial Library (1082), in 1117. Nothing is heard of the intendant's activities until 1144 when Ch'in Hsi was appointed to the position. The intendant is heard of again in 1221 when Chao I-fu was appointed to the position and 1254 when Yu Yü filled it. Judging from these data the position of

completed, but the result of the intendent's effort to acquire additional works appears to have been limited. Only two significant additions to the collections are noted in the sources, both in 1145. They were 756 *chüan* donated by a certain Ch'en Yang and fifty-one works donated by a Chang Lun.[9] No other major acquisitions are recorded in the sources for the next forty-five years, except the works produced by the scholarly agencies.

Coincidental with the meager post-1143 acquisition effort the number of directive personnel staff members began to decline markedly. The staff fell off to four or five members until the 1150's when it rose again. The increase which was sustained in varying degree through 1190, however, seems to have been more in response to the need for personnel to compile collections of documents and write histories than to attend to Imperial Library operations. The directive personnel staff did not again attain the number reached in the 1130's and early 1140's until 1190. Yet the absence of a full complement of directive personnel did not necessarily limit the use of the Imperial Library collections for, as we shall see, the operative personnel largely cared for them.

Thus by the time the Imperial Library moved into its new quarters in 1144 a significant portion of what would be its holdings in the Southern Sung appears to have been acquired and readied for use. Consequently the directive personnel staff diminished and never attained the height it had reached before 1144, its most important tasks already having been accomplished.

The Imperial Library reconstituted its holdings largely from private sources. With few exceptions it was the individual library owner who provided the desired works. Who owned these private libraries? How extensive were their holdings? How well collated were their texts? The private libraries known to have contributed works to the Imperial Library were all owned by persons in official circles. Moreover, most contributors were civil service personnel, that is scholar-officials. Geographically dispersed, but apparently aware of each other's activities by virtue of their role as officials, members of this group appear to have been easily made aware of the government's bibliographic needs.[10] Furthermore, they seem to have been predisposed to satisfy these needs by granting the government the privilege of making copies of their texts if they did not provide the originals.

Private library holdings probably varied greatly from a handful of books kept on a convenient shelf to a large collection which was carefully selected and cataloged. The catalogs of these private libraries which are extant indicate that they could grow to considerable proportions, often over several generations. Reports of the holdings of some large private libraries confirm this point. One catalog shows that the library contained 20,811 *chüan,* another 24,500 *chüan* (actually two collections combined), another 30,000 *chüan* and a final one approximately 49,700 *chüan.* These figures may be compared to those for the holdings of the Imperial Library: 30,669 *chüan* in the collection in 1041, 44,486 *chüan* in 1178 and 59,429 *chüan* in 1220.

The texts in private libraries appear to have been well collated as is suggested by the arguments in favor of the hand-copied text over the printed one advanced by the owner of a large Sung library, Yeh Meng-te.[11] First, when a work is reproduced by hand, he argues, each copy is collated in the process of copying; whereas wood-block printing reproduces many copies of a work without the benefit of collation for each one. Second, a scholar who hand-copies a text is likely to study it more thoroughly because of the difficulty by which it is obtained. In contrast, printed books are acquired more easily, therefore offering less incentive for collecting and studying.

Yeh Meng-te argues the merits of the hand-copied book from the point of view of the scholar to whom it was a precious item. Although one might question his argument, it does indicate the concern of the bibliophile for an accurate text. Textual criticism was the mainstay of Chinese scholarship, and quite possibly the interested owner hand-copied each text acquired, correcting it and studying it in the process. Sitting before a text he patiently brought his learning and skill to bear upon it. Under these conditions one might justifiably conclude that texts acquired by the Imperial Library from this source were apt to be accurate.

The Imperial Library acquired writings by making known its needs to bibliophiles in official circles, by sending directive personnel on scouting trips and by utilizing the administrative hierarchy of the government which extended throughout the empire. All these methods were used simultaneously and with varying degrees of effectiveness.

In the years 1131 and 1132 while the Imperial Library was in Shao-hsing prefecture all known contributions to the holdings of the newly activated agency came from individuals who were in official circles, if not directly affiliated with the government. For instance a certain Ho K'e-chung is credited with making the first contribution to the Imperial Library collections. He submitted a total of twenty-two volumes: four volumes of the *Reign Chronicle of Emperor T'ai Tsu* (*T'ai Tsu huang-ti shih-lu*), twelve volumes of

intendant was only filled intermittently. See *LTKS* 1/6a; *NSKKL*(1) 7/3a; *NSKKL*(2) 7/6b, 7/9a, 7/12a, 9/18a, 9/29a; *YH* 121/52a–52b; *SCSS* 9/15a; Li Hsin-ch'üan, *Chien-yen i-lai ch'ao-yeh tsa-chi* (in: *Wu-ying tien chü-chen pan ch'üan-shu,* 1899), 10/13a–13b. Hereafter cited as *CYTC.*

[9] *SHY:CJ* 4/27a–27b.

[10] *CHWC* 75/3a–3b discusses the practice of friends copying each other's texts. Additional evidence exists in the informal writings of bibliophiles.

[11] *SLYY* 8/5b–6a.

the *Precious Ennunciations of Sung Emperors* (*Kuo-ch'ao pao-shun*), three volumes of the *Biographies of Famous Officials* (*Ming-ch'en lieh-chuan*), and three volumes of the *Selected Documents of the Sung Dynasty* (*Kuo-ch'ao hui-yao*).[12] Several months later the widow of Chang Mou, a former general, presented 222 volumes from her husband's private library. The items singled out for mention from her contribution were the *Selected Documents of Six Reigns* (*Liu-ch'ao hui-yao*) and *Monographs from the Six Reign Histories* (*Liu-ch'ao kuo-shih chih*).[13] The *Selected Documents of the Sung Dynasty* in 300 *chüan*, re-edited by Wang Kuei, was submitted by a certain T'ang K'ai.[14] The final contribution known to have been made before the Imperial Library moved from Shao-hsing to Hang-chou consisted largely of 510 *chüan* of five reign chronicles from the collection of one Huang Meng.[15]

The Imperial Library moved to Hang-chou in 1132 where it stayed for the remainder of the Southern Sung. Persons in official circles who were also associated with the government continued to draw works from their private libraries for the Imperial Library. In 1132 Tseng Wen-fu, the son of a former Lesser Lord of the Imperial Sacrifices (*T'ai-ch'ang shao-ching*), contributed 2,678 *chüan*.[16] In the same year one Wei Hsü submitted the family copy of the *Writings of Emperor T'ai Tsung* (*T'ai Tsung huang-ti yü-shu*).[17] The administrator of Ching-chiang prefecture, Hsü Chung, submitted three works of the emperor in 1133. Two of these went to the Imperial Library.[18]

The Imperial Library also acquired works by sending staff members on scouting trips. The vice-director of the Imperial Library, Hung Hsi, made such a journey to various locales in south China soon after the move to Hang-chou. At Fu-chou he saw "reign histories" in the private library of Yü Shen and at Ch'üan-chou "reign chronicles" and other rare works in the private library of Chao T'ing. On returning to the capital he requested that arrangements be made to acquire these works or copies of them for the Imperial Library. Later that year Hung Hsi noted that an abundance of texts had been submitted as a result of his trip.[19]

Similarly on request Han Yü, a grandson of the famous Northern Sung minister Han Ch'i, provided the Imperial Library with a work entitled the *Erh-fu chung-i* in 1133. A copy was made at the Imperial Library and the original returned to the owner.[20] In the same vein an indeterminate number of "reign histories," "reign chronicles" and other works belonging to a former Imperial Library official were sent to the Imperial Library for copying as a result of the scouting efforts of the vice-director of the Imperial Library, Tseng T'ung.[21]

Contributions made by those in official circles and acquisitions by Imperial Library personnel on scouting trips were the most important means of gathering works from private sources, particularly in the period 1131 to 1135. Although the total number of works contributed is not known, it is clear from the number and size of individual acquisitions that these two methods produced startling results. The period of intense acquisition (1131–1135) seems to have satisfied the more pressing book needs of the Imperial Library. Consequently from 1136 to 1143 the full complement of directive personnel on duty probably busied themselves preparing the works gathered for the collections. No doubt the task of preparing the works was completed in 1143 for the Imperial Library was left with a skeleton staff too small to seek out large numbers of works directly; therefore utilization of the administrative hierarchy of government to gather works, a means in use before 1143, now became important. Acquisition in this manner had the advantage of covering the whole empire, being continuously in operation and calling on government personnel other than Imperial Library staff members.

The government was located in the capital city of Hang-chou, the apex of an administrative hierarchy which reached out from the capital to all prefectures, each of which supervised a handful of subprefectures (*hsien*). The latter were the basic units of government and the one closest to the people. Characteristically a subprefecture consisted of a town which was the administrative center and the surrounding villages. Early in the Northern Sung the population of a large subprefecture might exceed 4,000 households while a small one might have less than 500. The staff of an important subprefecture was usually headed by a subprefectural administrator (*chi-hsien*) who was responsible for the general welfare of the people, assisted by an assistant subprefect (*ch'eng*), a registrar (*chu-pu*), a sheriff (*wei*), and a clerical staff.[22] Several subprefectures were placed under the authority of one of four kinds of prefectures: superior (*fu*), ordinary

---

[12] *SHY:CJ* 4/20b. *NSKKL*(1) 3/1a gives the first three works only.
[13] *SHY:CJ* 4/21a; *NSKKL*(1) 3/1a.
[14] *SHY:CJ* 4/21a.
[15] *SHY:CJ* 4/21a. These include the *T'ai Tsu huang-ti shih-lu*, 50 *chüan*; *T'ai Tsung huang-ti shih-lu*, 80 *chüan*; *Shen Tsung huang-ti shih-lu*, 150 *chüan*; *Jen Tsung huang-ti shih-lu*, 200 *chüan*; *Ying Tsung huang-ti shih-lu*, 30 *chüan*. Another work in ten volumes, the *T'ien-sheng nan-chiao lu-pu ts'e-chi*, cannot be positively identified.
[16] *NSKKL*(1) 3/1a; *SHY:CJ* 4/22a.
[17] *SHY:CJ* 4/22a.
[18] *SHY:CJ* 4/23a–23b.
[19] *SHY:CJ* 4/22a–22b.

[20] *SHY:CJ* 4/22b.
[21] *SHY:CJ* 4/23a.
[22] Edward A. Kracke, Jr., *Civil Service in Early Sung China*, pp. 46–47. A detailed discussion of the topic is available in Brian E. McKnight, *Village and Bureaucracy in Southern Sung China* (Chicago, 1971).

(*chou*), military (*chün*) and industrial (*chien*). The head of a prefecture, known as an administrator (*chih*), was assisted in the case of large prefectures by one or two vice-administrators (*t'ung-p'an*) who supervised several civil aides (*mu-chih*). A corps of inspectors and clerks completed the staff.

Although the prefectures were linked directly to the government in Hang-chou, their operations were supervised by a corps of circuit intendants (*chien-ssu*) sent out from the capital. These intendants, often carrying instructions for local administrators, traveled fixed routes or circuits (*lu*) throughout the empire. One of their tasks was to search out writings for the Imperial Library in conjunction with locally based prefectural administrators. Aided by the circuit intendants and prefectural administrators, the Imperial Library could reach any village in the empire for works it desired.[23]

When the Imperial Library had intelligence of a work in private hands that it wished to acquire, instructions were given to the appropriate circuit intendant, who contacted the prefectural administrator in charge of the area and arranged for the work to be acquired or for the text to be transmitted to the Imperial Library where it was copied.[24] To illustrate, in 1132 a prefectural administrator completed arrangements for one Ho Lin to contribute 5,000 *chüan* from his private library. A year later the prefectural administrator of Hu-chou was asked to prevail upon a certain Lin Shu to obtain certain titles.[25] The arrangements were completed and in 1133 his son Lin Yen submitted seven rolls and 2,122 *chüan*.[26]

In addition to obtaining specific works from private sources through the administrative hierarchy the Imperial Library often requested that private library catalogs be transmitted to its offices. They were checked against the Imperial Library holdings and, if a desirable text was found, the appropriate circuit intendant was ordered to request the local prefectural administrator to secure the text or arrange for it to be copied at the capital.[27] Thus not only were the circuit intendants and prefectural administrators responsible for acquiring specific works, but for transmitting private library catalogs to be checked for desired items also.[28]

Finally the administrative hierarchy was instrumental in carrying out general imperial proclamations

calling for works for the Imperial Library from private sources. In 1135 the emperor proclaimed that schools and families in the various circuits, prefectures, and sub-prefectures be ordered to make available copies of works in their possession.[29] The response to this proclamation is not known, but potentially the Imperial Library could draw from every private source by means of its empire-wide network.

Contemporary scholarship also provided a limited number of significant works for the Imperial Library in addition to those produced by the scholarly agencies. Ch'eng Chü gave a copy of the *Lin-t'ai ku-shih,* a major source for the study of the Northern Sung Imperial Library.[30] A prefectural administrator from Szechwan, Li Shou-chih, submitted a copy of his *Commentaries on the Book of Changes* (*I-chieh*).[31] There are numerous examples of scholars presenting copies of their works to the Imperial Library; however, they are usually officials in the government.[32]

Contributions to the Imperial Library collections from private library owners were usually not gratuitous acts. A number of inducements had to be offered to elicit donations. The most important of these in the Northern Sung was money paid according to a plan enacted in 984. It stipulated that anyone contributing items on the Imperial Library want list to the extent of 300 *chüan* was to receive money and silk in appropriate quantities. Those who contributed 300 *chüan* or more were to have the opportunity of sending one member of the family to the Bureau of Academicians to be examined and considered for a position in the civil service.[33] This plan was reaffirmed in 993 except that donors of less than 300 *chüan* were to receive 1,000 cash (*ch'ien*) per *chüan,* rather than money and silk in appropriate quantities.[34] On at least two occasions in the Northern Sung considerable sums were expended for Imperial Library acquisitions. In 994, 100,000 cash was paid out for a collection. The list contained works of official historiography, including a portion of a "daily record" and the collected papers of several individuals.[35] In another case 300,000 cash was paid for a collection of 800 *chüan,* an average of 375 cash per *chüan.*[36]

The government south of the Yangtze River tried to revive this practice of paying for contributions made to the Imperial Library collections.[37] There is no evidence, however, that money was actually given out and it is quite likely that it was not, inasmuch as the

[23] Edward A. Kracke, Jr., *Civil Service in Early Sung China,* pp. 46–47.
[24] *NSKKL*(2) 3/16a.
[25] *SHY:CJ* 4/21b–22b.
[26] *SHY:CJ* 4/22b.
[27] *SHY:CJ* 2/23a. The works submitted were the *Tsu Tsung shih-lu,* the *Kuo-ch'ao hui-yao* and a *Kuo-shih.*
[28] *SHY:CJ* 4/24a and 26b. An alternative to this procedure was proposed in 1179. An official observed that there were many books in Szechwan and suggested that the Imperial Library send its catalog to be examined for items available in that region, but not included in its catalog. See *SHY:CJ* 4/31a.

[29] *SHY:CK* 18/27a–27b.
[30] *LTKS* Li/1a; *SHY:CJ* 5/30b.
[31] *SHY:CJ* 5/33a.
[32] *SHY:CJ* 5/40a; *CYTC* 4/11a.
[33] *LTKS* 2/1b–2a.
[34] *LTKS* 2/3a, 2/4b–5a.
[35] *SHY:CJ* 4/16b–17a.
[36] *SHY:CJ* 4/18a, *LTKS* 2/7a.
[37] See for examples *NSKKL*(1) 1/4b, *NSKKL*(2) 3/1b–2a, *SHY:CJ* 4/25b–26a, *SHY:CJ* 4/31a–31b.

government was never prosperous.[38] In lieu of cash the government offered remunerations which had cash value. In some cases contributors were given Ordination Certificates (*tu-tieh*). These were issued by the government to evidence the fact that the holder was a duly ordained Buddhist monk. Certification was felt to be necessary to control their numbers as they were partially exempt from taxation, labor services, and harsh punishments. More importantly Ordination Certificates were negotiable instruments. They were sold by the government and could be re-sold by the owner. In 1132 between 50,000 and 60,000 certificates were sold and between 1161 and 1170 an estimated 120,000. The official price for an Ordination Certificate in 1161 was 510 strings of cash, a figure which would rise to 700 by 1185.[39]

A donor could be well rewarded for his contribution to the Imperial Library by this means. In the case of the widow of Chang Mou mentioned above, she was given ten Ordination Certificates for her *222*-volume contribution. This was equivalent to about 5,100 strings of cash for the whole collection or twenty-three strings per volume.[40] The contribution of *520 chüan* by Huang Meng elicited five Ordination Certificates without names, thus ensuring their negotiability.[41]

Another form of remuneration offered to donors was a minimal status in the civil service. Again it was not a direct cash payment, but a reward which the government could give at will with no direct cost to itself and which would still materially benefit the recipient. The most common reward in this category was Classification Title 40 (CT 40). This was the lowest of forty classes into which directive officials were ranked. Along with Classification Title 39 (CT 39), it provided the holder with a minimal standing in the civil service, but no position.[42] Those who held Classification Title 40, however, were exempt from taxation, labor service, and harsh punishments.

On one occasion Classification Title 37 (CT 37) was given as a reward. This went to Wei Hsü, a person who had already passed the civil service examination.[43] Having qualified for a position by passing this examination, his contribution and subsequent reward of Classification Title 37 ensured him of an actual appointment to a position in the government. In two cases donors were given the position of Education Inspector of the prefecture (*Chou wen-hsüeh*), a low one in the

directive service.[44] No mention is made of their rank and perhaps they were in the nature of honorary appointments. These too carried exemption from taxation, labor service, and harsh punishment. To a donor who was already in the civil service the government often gave a transfer to a position which was higher on the protocol list than his rank in the service would normally command.[45] As in the two previous cases this form of reward did not require a cash outlay for the government.

These rewards appear to have been given for significant contributions and only if the text itself was given to the Imperial Library. On occasions when an individual would not give up a work despite a lucrative reward the government was content to make a copy at its own expense and perhaps offer a token reward.[46] This being done, the original was returned to its owner.

That members of the civil service and persons associated with the government were able to draw from their personal collections works which had been compiled or written in the scholarly agencies suggests that while the latter were dependent upon the private library to reconstitute their holdings early in the Southern Sung, at other times they were a source for bibliophiles. The three extant private catalogs from the Southern Sung list various works from this corpus of material.[47] Did officials arrange for copies of these works to be made for their private libraries? Quite possibly yes, although no explicit evidence has come to light to confirm this conclusion. Undoubtedly these works would have been desirable additions to a private collection, particularly to one owned by an official. In addition there seems to have been no specific restriction on duplicating these works and there were opportunities to do so.

Moreover, the works compiled and written in the scholarly agencies were usually kept in the Imperial Library and in a collection on the palace grounds. The latter collection might offer little opportunity for copying, but the other one was readily accessible to the staff. Furthermore, in the case of the Imperial Library we know that officials frequently violated the rule prohibiting the removal of texts in its collections from the premises.[48] Once outside the Imperial Li-

---

[38] James T. C. Liu, *Ou Yang Hsiu, An Eleventh-Century NeoConfucianist* (Stanford, 1967), p. 12.

[39] Kenneth K. S. Ch'en, *Buddhism in China, an Historical Survey* (Princeton, 1964), pp. 391–393. See also Robert des Rotours, *Traité des Fonctionnaires* 2: p. 482 for an explanation of *tu-tieh*.

[40] *SHY:CJ* 4/21a.

[41] *SHY:CJ* 4/21a.

[42] Edward A. Kracke, Jr., *Translation of Sung Civil Service Titles*, p. 4.

[43] *SHY:CJ* 4/22a.

[44] *SHY:CJ* 4/20b, 4/24a–24b; Edward A. Kracke, Jr., *Civil Service in Early Sung China*, pp. 48–49 and 235.

[45] See for examples *SHY:CJ* 4/21a, 4/27a. See also Robert des Rotours, *Traité des Fonctionnaires* 1: pp. 50–51, n. 4.

[46] *SHY:CJ* 4/25a, 4/27a, 5/33a, 6/15a. On one occasion *yung-mien wen-chieh* was given as a reward. See *SHY:CJ* 4/27b. This might be understood as "eternally exempt from the prefectural examination." That is, the contributor was given a pass on the first of the three civil service examinations.

[47] See for examples Yu Mou, *Sui-ch'u t'ang-shu-mu* (in: *Hai-shan hsien-kuan ts'ung-shu*, 1849), 1/11a–12a, 1/16a, 1/36b. Hereafter cited as *SCT*.

[48] *NSKKL(2)* 3/2a–2b. This problem of illegal borrowing was prevalent in the Northern Sung also. See for examples *LTKS* 2/4a, 2/7a–7b, 2/9a.

brary building complex they could be copied at will. The flow of writings from private library to Imperial Library, then, was probably only one-half of a cycle of exchange. Copies of government texts, including those of the Imperial Library, appear to have found their way into the collections of interested bibliophiles and back again when the need arose.

While private libraries provided most of the works necessary to reconstitute the Imperial Library collections, the government added to the collection also, but principally new works. Imperial writings bulk large in this source of material. As noted above, Sung emperors created repositories for their predecessor's papers. These probably received the bulk of such material. Nevertheless, a limited number of pieces appear to have been deposited in the Imperial Library, particularly those which were in the nature of state papers. Although limited in quantity, the writings of emperors added an important element to the Imperial Library holdings.

Perhaps the most significant government additions to the Imperial Library collections were the compilations of documents and the written histories. These were often large works, running to 1,000 *chüan* and 2,000 *chüan* in some cases. Moreover, 300 *chüan* and 400 *chüan* works were not uncommon. When one considers that the total Imperial Library collection ready for use did not exceed 50,000 *chüan,* an addition of 500 *chüan* was a substantial one.

The Directorate of Education was a source of printed works for the Imperial Library. The texts it printed were largely authorized versions of standard writings, in many cases collated in the scholarly agencies.[49] As early as the Han dynasty the government assumed the responsibility for providing the public with officially prepared editions of the canonical and other standard texts. These were regularly carved on stone tablets and arranged in a place where the public had access to them.[50] An individual could compare his text with the one prepared by the government or make an ink squeeze copy for himself. In this manner these works were distributed.

This practice continued to be followed until recent times. In the middle of the tenth century, however, the Directorate of Education began the practice of having wooden printing blocks carved for officially approved editions of works. Now in addition to acquiring copies of works by means of ink squeezing, personal copies of wood-block-printed editions of them could be had on request for the cost of materials.[51] This was a continuation of the government practice of making publicly available copies of well-edited editions of texts,

but by the "modern" technology of wood-block printing. Printed editions were obtained by the Imperial Library either directly from the Directorate of Education or indirectly from private collectors.[52] The number of items acquired in this manner cannot be estimated in the absence of full data.

Another limited source of writings for the Imperial Library in the Sung was interagency copying. As a rule works destined for the government were first presented to the emperor who passed them on to the proper agency. On occasion an agency acquired a work which the Imperial Library wanted to add to its collections. In these cases the latter agency made a copy of it. Thus in 1131 some papers of Ou-yang Hsiu, an outstanding scholar of the Northern Sung, were presented to the Court of Imperial Sacrifices, and the Imperial Library made a copy of them for its collections.[53]

Finally local units of government also appear to have contributed works to the Imperial Library. Attention has already been drawn to the role of the administrative network of the government in gathering works for the Imperial Library from private sources. It was also used to gather works from local units of government. In 1144 the emperor proclaimed that prefectures should make a copy of each work for which they held printing blocks. These were to be printed on yellow paper and sent up to the Imperial Library.[54] The number of books obtained in this manner is unknown, but presumably some titles were acquired over the years.

PROCESSING OF WORKS FOR THE COLLECTIONS

The books acquired for the Imperial Library collections were put through an elaborate process before they were ready for use. In 1177 almost one-third (32 per cent) of the Imperial Library collections were as yet unprocessed. Another 8.5 per cent were printed works which required little attention before they were placed in their special collection. The remaining 59.5 per cent of the books, that is the main collection and the Imperial Archives collection, were manuscript copies which were thoroughly examined and emended before they were copied and allowed to be used.

An instance of acquisition and preparation will illustrate the process. Upon receipt of 2,678 *chüan* from the private library of Tseng Min in 1132, the temporary vice-director of the Imperial Library, Wang Ang, memorialized the emperor to the effect that these works had not been collated and emended as was required by the rules. The first step in the procedure he outlined was to arrange the items into the fourfold classifications scheme. This having been done, an es-

[49] Wang Kuo-wei, *Wu-tai liang-sung chien-pen k'ao* (in: *Hai-ning wang-ching-an hsien-sheng i-shu,* 1936).

[50] Tsien Tsuen-hsuin, *Written on Bamboo and Silk,* pp. 73–79.

[51] *SHY:CK* 28/1a. See also Yeh Te-hui, *Shu-lin ch'ing-hua* (*Sao-yeh shan-fang,* 1920) 6/1a–3a, 6/3a–3b.

[52] *SHY:CJ* 4/25b, *SHY:CK* 18/6b.

[53] *SHY:CJ* 5/30b. For additional examples see *SHY:CJ* 5/33a–34a.

[54] *SHY:CK* 18/27a–27b.

timate of the work involved was made and appropriate directive personnel were assigned from the Imperial Library staff to examine and collate the texts. Usually this was done by the collators and correctors of the Imperial Library, but for Imperial Archives texts special temporary appointees (*Hsing-chu kuan*) could be assigned. Persons involved in this type of work were expected to prepare twenty-one leaves a day.[55] The person who did the work was required to sign his name at the end of each *chüan*. A record of each person's daily accomplishment was kept by his superior. At the end of each ten-day period a preliminary report was sent to the director of the Imperial Library. A monthly sealed report was made to the director also, possibly for transmission to the Department of Ministries.[56]

The care taken to standardize processing procedures is further exemplified by the rules for collation posted outside the offices of the collators and correctors of the Imperial Library. These rules gave explicit step-by-step procedures to follow for a variety of situations.[57] That the rules were openly displayed for all persons on the premises to see suggests that they were actually followed.

After the directive personnel completed their task, the texts were turned over to the Copyist Office (*Pu-hsieh so*), an operative personnel office. The copyists and correctors among the Imperial Library operative personnel served concurrently in the Copyist Office. Here they were billeted as *Shu-hsieh k'ai-shu*,[58] that is, copyists. As with the directive personnel serving as collators and correctors, the operative personnel had to conform to well-defined work regulations. They were expected to copy 2,000 characters a day; however, in winter, perhaps when hands, ink, and brush were stiff with cold, this daily quota was lowered to 1,500 characters a day.[59] When an extraordinarily large number of works were to be copied additional persons were hired. Thus in 1178 the Imperial Library reported that the collections had been corrected and copied as ordered. In the process a total of 50,000,000 characters had been recopied by hired copyists at a cost of one string of cash (*sheng-kuan*) per 10,000 characters.[60] The total cost was 5,000 strings of cash. This undertaking would have required ninety-two men one year to complete if they worked at the assigned rate of 2,000 characters a day for nine days out of each ten for nine months (spring, summer, and autumn) and at a rate of 1,500 characters a day for nine

out of ten days for the remaining three months (winter).[61]

The manuscript copies among the Imperial Library holdings, that is, the main collection and the Imperial Archives collection, appear to have been prepared in a uniform format. Books destined for the Imperial Archives were copied on yellow paper, the imperial color, with border and column marker lines. The covers for each volume were made of a yellow silk with a label made of blue-green silk on the cover of each volume. Each volume also had a yellow silk label protruding from it in a manner that permitted it to be seen when it was placed on a shelf. A number of volumes were wrapped together in a silk cloth to which a location tag made of sandalwood was attached. Finally the wrapped volumes were placed in the proper cabinet.[62] The texts in the main collection also appear to have been prepared in a uniform manner, but perhaps on different material and in different colors. On at least one occasion there is a suggestion that texts in the main collection were done on white paper.[63]

Care was taken to ensure the preservation of the books in the Imperial Library collections. The covers and end papers were treated with a special dye which repelled worms as had been done in the Northern Sung and earlier. The books were placed in cabinets, perhaps lined with camphor wood, which discouraged worms and held to a minimum of rough handling.[64] The books were aired each year for a short time in the summer. The airing period extended from the first day of the lunar fifth month to the first day of the lunar seventh month.[65] A brief airing in this period was probably sufficient to dry out the books and add substantially to their life.

CHARACTERISTICS OF THE COLLECTIONS

The Southern Sung Imperial Library holdings consisted of four collections, each housed separately in the building complex. These totaled an estimated *72,567 chüan* in 21,359 volumes.[66] The main collection, ar-

[55] The term used for leaf is *pan*, meaning a wooden printing block. Each printing block contained two pages which were printed on a single sheet of paper.
[56] *SHY:CJ* 4/13b; *NSKKL*(1) 3/1b; *YH* 43/23b.
[57] *NSKKL*(1) 3/2b–3a.
[58] *NSKKL*(1) 10/3b; *SHY:CK* 18/27b–28a.
[59] *NSKKL*(1) 10/3b; *SHY:CK* 18/27b–28a.
[60] *SHY:CK* 18/37b. See also Yang Lien-sheng, *Money and Credit in China, a Short History* (Cambridge, 1952), pp. 36–37 for an explanation of the term "string of cash."
[61] The *Pu-hsieh so* apparently was established for the first time during the Sung in 1074. See *NSKKL*(1) 3/2a; *SHY: CK* 18/4a–4b. In the Southern Sung it was in operation again in 1144. See *NSKKL*(1) 3/2a; *YH* 163/30a.
[62] *NSKKL*(1) 3/3a–3b.
[63] *LTKS* 2/7b.
[64] *LTKS* 2/7b. See also Laurence Sickman and Alexander Soper, *The Art and Architecture of China* (Baltimore, 1956), p. 180. Ths plate shows a "sutra cupboard" which may have been the manner in which books were stored in the Southern Sung Imperial Library.
[65] *NSKKL*(1) 3/1b–2a; *SHY:CK* 18/27a. These are the summer months.
[66] See table 6. Exact figures are given for the number of *chüan* in each section of the Imperial Library except for those kept in the second story of the Pi Ko; however, for this latter group we do have the number of volumes housed there. By multiplying the number of volumes housed in the second story of the Pi Ko (1,098) by 3.4, the average number of *chüan* per volume in all other cases and the approximate number in

ranged according to the fourfold classification system, was housed in the southern ends of the east and west lateral buildings [67] (see figs. 4, 7, and 8). Each of the four classes was provided with a separate five-module depository, two in the south end of each lateral building. The books were kept in cabinets, seven in each of the four depositories.[68]

The Imperial Archives collection, totaling an estimated 19,741 *chüan* in 5,670 volumes, was another significant segment of the Imperial Library holdings. This collection consisted primarily of state papers.[69] Other writings may have been included here as well, as is suggested by its arrangement according to the fourfold classification system.[70] The collection was housed on the second floor of the Imperial Archives [71] and in two depositories, one in the east lateral building and another in the west one. The east depository had three modules and the west depository two. Each contained eight cabinets to house the books [72] (see tables 5 and 6).

The Imperial Archives was not the central agency for housing documents. As noted above, the emperor's writings were in large part kept in imperial repositories in the palace grounds. Thus, the Imperial Archives was a select collection of imperial papers.

A third collection consisted of printed books. It totaled 6,098 *chüan* in 1,721 volumes.[73] These printed books were obtained from private persons and agencies of local government as well as the Directorate of Education. That printed books were both included in the Imperial Library holdings and housed separately is not difficult to understand. Since the tenth century, the technology of wood-block printing appears to have been used with greater frequency in producing books. Although a scholar of note such as Yeh Meng-te might

TABLE 5

IMPERIAL LIBRARY BOOK SPACE BY COLLECTION, MODULE, AND CABINET[a]

Collection	Number of cabinets for each collection	Average number of volumes per cabinet	Number of modules per collection	Average number of cabinets per module
Main collection	28	233	20	1.4
Imperial archives	16	286	5	3.2
Printed books	7	246	3	2.3
Unprocessed works	[29]	[255]	5	5.8

[a] Data drawn from *NSKKL*(1) 2/1b–7b.

each case, we arrive at an estimate of the number of *chüan* in the volumes stored there. It is 3,733 *chüan*.

[67] Tsuen-hsuin Tsien, "A History of Bibliographic Classification in China," *Library Quart.* 22 (1952): pp. 311–314.
[68] *NSKKL*(1) 2/4a–5a.
[69] *NSKKL*(1) 2/2a–2b, 2/4a, 2/4b.
[70] *NSKKL*(1) 3/3a–3b.
[71] *NSKKL*(1) 2/2a–2b.
[72] *NSKKL*(1) 2/4a–4b.
[73] *NSKKL*(1) 2/4b.

TABLE 6

PRINCIPAL IMPERIAL LIBRARY COLLECTIONS AND THEIR LOCATIONS[a]

Collection	Location[b]	Number of *chüan*	Number of volumes[c]
Main collection	10 and 11	23,583	6,512
Imperial archives	7, 10, and 11	19,741 (est.)[d]	5,670
Printed books	11	6,098	1,721
Unprocessed works	14	23,145	7,456
Totals		72,567 (est.)	21,359

[a] *Pi-ko chu-k'u shu-mu.* Source *NSKKL*(1) 3/3a–4a. *YH* 52/43b gives the same data. In addition to its holdings of writings, the Imperial Library held 2 volumes and 911 rolls of paintings, 1 volume and 126 rolls of calligraphy, 418 ancient vessels, 75 ink stones, and 7 lutes.
[b] Location symbols refer to fig. 4: Sketch plan of the Imperial Library Building Complex.
[c] The usual practice in the Sung of giving the number of *chüan* for a work or a collection is supplemented in the case of this working catalog by giving the number of volumes in which these *chüan* are contained. That the character *chüan* should not be read in its basic meaning of "roll" is suggested by the presence of a volume (*ts'e*) figure after each *chüan* figure which stand in a ratio to each other of about 1:3.4 in each case. Moreover, the description given of the format in which manuscript copies of books were prepared for the collections is of a volume.
[d] The Imperial Archives collection is a bit more complicated than the other three. First, in addition to 5,670 volumes it contains 607 rolls (*chou*) and 5 odd sheets (*tao*) which were preserved because they were in the hand of an emperor. See *NSKKL*(2) 3/2b where they are described, in addition to the source from which they and this whole table were drawn, *NSKKL*(1) 3/3a–4a. In addition, the elements which made up the Imperial Archives collection are given as follows:
1. 35 volumes of administrative orders in the hand of the emperor (*yü-cha*) located on the second floor of the Imperial Archives (7).
2. 61 volumes of imperial orders (*T'ai-shang huang-ti sheng-cheng*) located on the second floor of the Imperial Archives (7).
3. 1,002 volumes of the 'daily record' located on the second floor of the Imperial Archives (7). Although the number of volumes is given for each of these three elements, no *chüan* figure is given. It is quite possible that these works were not divided into *chüan*. However, for the sake of consistency in this table we have estimated the number of *chüan* on the basis of 3.4 to 1.
4. 13,506 *chüan* is 3,958 volumes arranged according to the fourfold classification system and located in the east and west lateral building (10 and 11).
5. 2,502 *chüan* in 614 volumes of writings written in the presence of the emperor, arranged according to the fourfold classification system and located in the east and west lateral building (10 and 11).

prefer a manuscript copy of a text, the printed book had distinct advantages. It was probably cheaper to acquire, easier to find in the market and, if necessary, could be had in multiple copies. Moreover, the demand for books made it profitable for the commercial publishers to supplement the works of government and private printers. The Imperial Library evidently retained the printed texts it acquired in the original form, perhaps adding a *chüan* of corrections. Yet they were still regarded with less esteem than the manuscript copy, the form in which texts in the main collection and Imperial Archives were prepared. The time when the Sung printed book would be valued over the manuscript copy was still to come. But the printed books selected for acquisition by the Imperial Library were probably sound texts and printed well, particularly in the case of works from the Directorate of Education.

A fourth group of works were items not yet prepared for use. These were housed in a five-module depository in the Selected Documents Office.[74] This collection is not explicitly identified as unprocessed works, but there is sufficient evidence to justify such a conclusion. First, it was called the *sou-fang* depository (*sou-fang k'u*). The term *sou-fang* means "to search and investigate" and is used in the sources to indicate the gathering of books for the Imperial Library.[75] Thus works gathered were stored in this unit after acquisition. In time they were prepared for use and placed in one of the collections. These works, however, which were as yet unprocessed, including perhaps duplicate and extraneous works, were simply left here. Consequently, when the catalog was compiled in 1177, it was found that 23,145 *chüan* in 7,456 volumes were housed in the *sou-fang* depository. That these were works gathered from the empire is clear from the former name of the *sou-fang* depository, the *T'i Chü So Shu K'u* which means the "writings depository of the Intendant's office." [76] The intendant was in charge of gathering works for the Imperial Library.

Further indication of the nature of the writings in the *sou-fang* depository is given by its location and size (see table 5). It was situated north of the section of the building complex given over to the Imperial Library's creative and processing activities, in the Compilation Hall and adjacent buildings. Not only was this collection removed from the proximity of the Imperial Library, but it also appears to have been kept in quarters of minimal adequacy. There is no mention of cabinets being provided for the books as in the case of the other three collections. Perhaps the writings were just piled on shelves in the *sou-fang* depository, rather than put in cabinets, the normal way of storing writings ready for use. However, even if we assume that cabinets were provided, it would appear that the space allotted was much more restricted than for the other three collections. The number of volumes per cabinet averaged 255 for the first three collections. There was a difference of only 55 volumes per cabinet. This suggests a similar size cabinet for all three collections. If we assume that a *sou-fang* cabinet is capable of holding 255 volumes, it would have required a minimum of twenty-nine cabinets to

hold the total of 7,456 volumes in the collection. The twenty-nine cabinets would be arranged in five modules for an average of almost six cabinets per module. This is nearly twice the number of cabinets per module for the Imperial Archives which had an average of three per module, the greatest number among the three collections. Moreover, if we assume that the *Chung-hsing kuan-ko shu-mu* includes all works in the collection, exclusive of unprocessed items, then this, too, is further indication that the works in the *sou-fang* depository were not fully incorporated into it. The *Chung-hsing kuan-ko shu-mu* lists 44,489 *chüan*. If we deduct the number of *chüan* in the *sou-fang* depository from the estimated total in the *Pi-ko chu-k'u shu-mu*, the union catalog of Imperial Library holdings, we arrive at a figure of 49,422. Allowing for some duplicates in the printed books collection, we approximate the total in the Imperial Library catalog of 1178, that is, 44,486 *chüan*.

The principal goal of the Imperial Library was to reconstitute its holdings as they had been in the Northern Sung, with high priority given to the acquisition of works produced by the scholarly agencies. To this end the *Ch'ung-wen tsung-mu*, a union catalog of the holdings of the Ch'ung Wen Library published in 1043, was circulated among local officials early in the Southern Sung.[77] On another occasion the bibliographic section of the standard history of the T'ang, an even older list, was circulated.[78] Beyond this, in 1147 the historian Cheng Ch'iao examined the Imperial Library collection for the missing items. The outcome of his investigation was a list of desiderata, *Ch'iu-shu hs'üeh-chi*.[79] He, too, appears to have been interested in works not yet held by the Imperial Library, but which were published prior to the Southern Sung.

The degree of selectivity suggested by the circulation of these lists appears to have been extended to works published in the Southern Sung also. While no precise statement of acquisition policy has come down to us, it is evident from the authors and titles listed in the two partially complete Southern Sung Imperial Library catalogs that the only works selected for inclusion were those of a high caliber of scholarship. Evidently the goal of the Imperial Library was to conserve the most noteworthy works of scholarship circulating in the Sung era, these to facilitate the conduct of government and foster scholarship.

It would be interesting to analyze the collections in terms of their subject content, literary or scholarly form, and relative emphasis on contemporary and older works. The incompleteness of the catalogs preserved to us limits such analyses, but we can at least form a rather general picture. The main collection was ar-

[74] *NSKKL*(1) 2/5a.
[75] *NSKKL*(2) 3/1b–2a.
[76] *NSKKL*(1) 2/5a.

[77] *SHY:CJ* 4/26a.
[78] *SHY:CJ* 4/26a.
[79] *YH* 52/42b; Chao Shih-wei (comp.), *Chung-hsing kuan-ko shu-mu chi-k'ao* (Peking, 1933), 3/18a. Hereafter cited as *NSKKSM*.

TABLE 7

SIZE OF SUNG LIBRARY COLLECTIONS AS INDICATED BY THEIR CATALOGS[a]

Catalog date	Number of *chüan*		
	Imperial Library[b]	T'ai Ch'ing library[c]	Private libraries[d]
1007	—	24,192	—
1041	30,669	—	—
ca. 1050	—	—	20,811[e]
1061	—	33,725	—
ca. 1090	—	—	30,000[f]
ca. 1117	—	—	—
—	—	45,018	—
1151	—	—	24,500[g]
1178	44,486	—	—
1220	59,429	—	—
ca. 1250	—	—	49,700[h]

[a] A difficulty peculiar to the assessment of the size of libraries arises from the different types of totals given for collections. This was noted by L. Carrington Goodrich in Thomas F. Carter, *The Invention of Printing in China and its Spread Westward*, pp. 42–43, n. 1 and des Rotours, *Traité des Fonctionnaires* 1: p. 191, n. 2; p. 206, n. 4. A case occurs where this ambiguity is clearly revealed in connection with the Southern Sung Imperial Library. The *Pi-ko chu-k'u shu-mu*, a union catalog of Imperial Library holdings and probably the working catalog dated 1177, gives an estimated total of 72,567 *chüan*. This may be compared with 44,486 *chüan* in the *Chung-hsing kuan-ko shu-mu*, the published catalog of the Imperial Library, compiled in 1177. The latter catalog was probably drawn from the former and the difference in the figures perhaps represents unprocessed works and some duplicates and extraneous works included in the former, but not in the latter. An indiscriminate use of these figures could substantially alter one's conception of the size of the Imperial Library's holdings. It is the figures for published catalogs which have been used in table 7 for comparative purposes since they represent the usable part of the collection, if not the whole, and they are the ones most easily judged to be of the same type so that one compares like things.

[b] The *Ch'ung-wen tsung-mu* was the first of four published catalogs of the Sung Imperial Library. It was compiled by Wang Yao-ch'en and others and formally submitted to Emperor Jen Tsung in 1041. See *LTKS* 3/7a–8a; *YH* 52/38a and 43a; *TK* 207/8a; *SHY:CK* 18/15a; *SLCT* 8/5a.

The second catalog of the Imperial Library, *Pi-shu tsung-mu*, was in the process of compilation about 1117, but only brief mention of it is made in these sources. Southern Sung references to a Northern Sung Imperial Library catalog are always to the *Ch'ung-wen tsung-mu*, also suggesting that the project was never completed. This is a strong likelihood in view of the renewed disturbances on the northern border. See *YH* 52/41b–42a and *SHY:CK* 18/19a.

The *Chung-hsing kuan-ko shu-mu* was the first published catalog of the Southern Sung Imperial Library collections. In 1176 the vice-director of the Imperial Library, Ch'en K'uei, and several other officials noted that no Imperial Library catalog has been compiled since the beginning of the Northern Sung. Permission was granted to execute the work and in 1178 the *Chung-hsing kuan-ko shu-mu* was formally presented to the emperor. See *NSKKL*(2) 4/1a; *YH* 52/43b; *SHY:CK* 18/37a.

The fourth Imperial Library catalog, *Chung-hsing kuan-ko hsü-shu-mu*, was submitted to the emperor in 1220. See *NSKKL*(2) 4/7b; *YH* 52/44a; a *SLCT* 8/10a–10b; *TK* 174/38a–38b.

[c] The T'ai Ch'ing Library was erected in 979. Emperor Chen Tsung put some papers in it written in the hand of his predecessor, Emperor T'ai Tsung. This appears to be the first time the build-

TABLE 7 CONTINUED

ing was put to use as a library. See *YH* 52/34a. It continued to be used as a library, but not as the imperial repository for the papers of Emperor T'ai Tsung. This function was carried on by the Lung T'u Ko. See table 1. The T'ai Ch'ing Library appears to have developed as a near duplicate of the Imperial Library collections for the personal use of the emperor and perhaps for safety in case of fire. In 999 the emperor ordered that the three institutes' staff copy the works in the main collection of the Ch'ung Wen Library. When completed they were transferred to the T'ai Ch'ing Library. See *YH* 52/34a–34b; *SHY:CJ* 4/1b–2a. Another copy was ordered to be made and placed in the Lung T'u Ko but there is no indication that this was done. In 1004 the three institutes staff submitted 24,162 *chüan*. See *YH* 52/34b. This appears to be the full installment of the copying project and the collection. Three years later we have record of a visit by Emperor Shen Tsung to the T'ai Ch'ing Library. At this time its collection had grown slightly to the figure indicated in this table, 24,192 *chüan*. However, we should note that *YH* 52/34a and *YH* 33/20b–21a both give the number of *chüan* in each section of the main collection. These total 24,192; however, the total given in these two sources is 25,192 *chüan*. Perhaps this is an error in addition. Also Li Tao, *Hsü Tzu-chih t'ung-chien ch'ang-pien*, 65/52a, gives 33,725 *chüan* under the year 1007, the same figure given in *YH* 164/20b for the year 1061. The latter source would appear to be correct in view of the progression of figures upward over time. The second figure is dated 1061. The figure of 45,018 *chüan* is for some indeterminate date, but still in the Northern Sung as this collection was carried off by the Jurchen in 1127 and there is no indication that it was reconstituted in the Southern Sung.

[d] A great deal of information on notable private libraries may be found in Yang Li-ch'ang and Chin Pu-ying, *Chung-kuo ts'ang-shu chia-k'ao lüeh* (1929) and Yeh Ch'ang-ch'in, *Ts'ang-shu chi-shih shih* (in: *Ling-chien ko ts'ung-shu*).

[e] This catalog, the *Han-tan shu-chih*, was compiled about the middle of the eleventh century. It was the private library of Li Pu. See *YH* 52/41a.

[f] This is the *T'ien-shih shu-mu*, the catalog of the family library compiled by T'ien Hao. It was completed in the period 1086–1094. See *TK* 207/10a.

[g] This catalog, the *Chün-chai tu-shu chih*, dated 1151, is for the library of Ch'ao Kung-wu. It is actually two collections brought together by a fortuitous friendship. See *SLCT* 8/9b.

[h] This catalog, the *Chih-chai shu-lu chieh-t'i*, dated about 1250, was compiled by Ch'en Chen-sun and records the contents of the largest single private collection known in the Sung.

ranged, then as in later times, according to the four-division scheme of canonical writings, history, philosophy, and literary collections. The numbers of volumes in the four divisions seem to have been rather similar.

The canonical writings consisted primarily of ancient works approved by Confucius or his followers (described earlier) touching on such diverse matters as philosophy, history, ritual, and divination, and secondarily, of later and contemporary commentaries on these. History consisted of works treating all periods from early times to very recent; it dealt not only with annals and general treatments of different periods, but also with governmental documents, specialized discussions of political institutions, and a broad range of matters that concerned the government, from early times to contemporary. Philosophy included speculations by thinkers other than Confucius and his principal early followers, and extended into discussions of mathematics, science, and technology. Literary collections included collected poems and papers of individual writers, or selected writings of particular groups of writers. Writings won a place in this category primarily for their esteemed style in the literary Chinese idiom, but the pieces ranged from a very generous representation of poetry in different forms, through essays and personal letters, to a large number of governmental papers by well-known writers.

It is obvious that the Imperial Library was catholic in its content; the most conspicuous gap (to our modern way of thinking) was perhaps the absence of dramatic or fictional writings in the vernacular language. These forms of literature were indeed already beginning to develop in this period, but had not yet emerged in advanced forms.

The Imperial Library was probably the largest single collection in the Southern Sung (see table 7). One may assume with a fair degree of probability that the 44,486 *chüan* listed in the *Chung-hsing kuan-ko shu-mu,* the catalog of the Imperial Library compiled and printed in the period 1177–1178, represent all its holdings processed and ready for use. These exclude a number of unprocessed works as well as possible duplicates and extraneous items. How large was the Imperial Library in relation to other Sung governmental libraries? The data are very limited. We have catalog figures for one of the palace libraries, the T'ai Ch'ing Library mentioned earlier. In 1007 the *Catalog of the T'ai Ch'ing Library* (*T'ai-ch'ing lou shu-mu*) listed a total of 24,192 *chüan.* This figure grew to 33,725 *chüan* in 1061 and to 45,018 at some indeterminately later date, but in the Northern Sung. These figures indicate that the collections were only slightly smaller than those of the Imperial Library in the Northern and Southern Sung. In 1015 a fire destroyed the holdings of the Imperial Library, a collection of some 36,280 *chüan.*[80] The T'ai Ch'ing Library was two-thirds the size of this eight years earlier by 1041, but two decades later the collection had grown several thousand *chüan* larger. Undoubtedly the Imperial Library had grown in the intervening twenty years also, making them about equal in size. The third figure we have for the size of the T'ai Ch'ing Library indicates that late in the Northern Sung its collection was slightly larger than the Imperial Library would become in 1178 and three-fourths the size it would attain in 1220.

The comparison of the size of the Sung Imperial Library collections with the Northern Sung T'ai Ch'ing Library holdings suggests that at least this one government library could approximate it in size; however, this appears to be the only one with which it could compare. A mid-eleventh century *Catalog of the Institute of History* (*Ta Sung shih-kuan shu-mu*) indicates that its collection was one-third the size of the

1220. The works listed in this catalog, however, were probably part of the Ch'ung Wen Library and as such only suggestive of relative size.

Thus among governmental libraries the T'ai Ch'ing Library is the only separate collection known to approximate the size of the Imperial Library and this perhaps because it was a near duplicate of the latter collection for the personal use of the emperor and for safety in case of fire. Judging from this comparison the Imperial Library was the most significant one in the government.

Relative to other library collections in Chinese society, can the Southern Sung Imperial Library still be regarded as the most important single library? Probably yes. Three of the four figures we have for the size of private libraries in the Sung indicate that they could reach half the size of the Imperial Library and in one case almost approximate it; however, these were probably among the largest private libraries in Sung China. The Imperial Library was surely far larger than the overwhelming number of private libraries and at least slightly larger than the largest.

Although the data in table 7 are limited, there is at least the suggestion of a trend toward larger collections: understandably, since the spread of education among new elements in society and the consequent demand for more books fostered the increased use of wood-block printing, not only for school books, but also for other titles of interest to a literate public.

While the Imperial Library was probably the largest single collection in Sung China and far larger than most personal collections, it should not obscure the fact that, without the private libraries to draw on, its holdings, which were periodically destroyed and dispersed, would have suffered in size and quality. The private libraries were a vast storehouse of scholarship, one which the Imperial Library could tap with confidence. Yet one should also recognize the role of the government as a source of writings for the private libraries. The two, responding to each other's needs, conserved a substantial body of significant documents and scholarly works.

THE USE OF THE COLLECTIONS

Use of the Imperial Library collections was supervised by members of the Imperial Library staff assigned on a rotating basis. The system of supervision was altered periodically but the basic scheme seems to have remained the same. Each book storage unit had an attendant (*K'u-tzu*) chosen on a daily basis from among the operative personnel.[81] The attendants were responsible to a director of attendants (*Chien-k'u-tzu*) who was chosen from among the directive personnel and also served on a daily basis. This official was simultaneously in charge of the bursary office (*Kung-shih-k'u*). Beyond this another of the direc-

---

[80] *YH* 52/31b–32a; *LTKS* 2/5b.

[81] *NSKKL*(1) 10/2b.

tive personnel was assigned on a monthly rotating basis to examine the collections. He appears to have been in charge of inspecting the physical condition of the books.[82]

The rotating responsibility for circulation and inspection by Imperial Library personnel suggests a need for security measures to protect the holdings from misuse or improper borrowing. Procedures governing collection use were clearly delineated. When an official wanted to use a text he first went to the Tao Shan Assembly Hall and requested use of the *Pi-ko chu-k'u shu-mu*, the *Union Catalog of the Imperial Library*. He was given this on signing his name. After he had used it, the catalog was locked up again.[83] Next he went to the appropriate book depository and requested the work he desired from the attendant.[84]

This well-designed system of procedures regulating access to the catalog and the rotating system for supervision indicates quite clearly that use of the Imperial Library was anticipated on a regular basis. The extent to which the collection was used, however, is difficult to assess. According to the regulations, an official could use them in the course of his duties, but only within the confines of the Imperial Library building complex.[85] With such an arrangement it was perhaps not necessary to keep elaborate records of collection use. We have no evidence that such records existed.

Undoubtedly the main users of the Imperial Library collections were officials engaged in scholarly agency projects. Their work was carried out in the ample space provided in the building complex. Perhaps only occasionally were the more comprehensive Imperial Library collections consulted by officials other than those engaged in the compilation of documents and the writing of histories. This is plausible, as agencies maintained small collections of books for their own needs and is further suggested by the absence of any general reading room.

The extent to which the Imperial Library was used for private research is difficult to estimate. Occasionally individual scholars seem to have received specific permission to use the collection, continuing the Northern Sung practice of access to imperial collections that had furthered Ssu-ma Kuang's great historical project. It is not certain that such permission was granted widely or as a matter of course. Nevertheless, in the Southern Sung scholars seem to have used the Imperial Library collections for personal research without the extraordinary permission of the emperor and on occasion perhaps in conflict with the rule prohibiting books from being removed from the Imperial Library building complex. Books were in fact taken from the complex as is evidenced by the several complaints registered by directive personnel in memorials throughout the Sung. Once outside the building complex the works could be copied for a private collection. It would appear that the Southern Sung scholars did use the collections.

Li Hsin-ch'uan, author of two great extant histories, is an apparent case of a prominent figure who used the Imperial Library collection for personal scholarship. Both of his works were written before he joined the civil service in 1231. His private scholarship seems to have qualified him for the special examination which gave him the status of one who passed the triennial civil service examination and a position in the government. He served much of the time in these scholarly agencies. As a member of the Imperial Library staff, he served as director, vice-director, executive-assistant, and assistant staff author. In addition he was a member of the commission which compiled the *Reign Histories and Reign Chronicles for Four Reigns* (*Ssu-ch'ao kuo-shih shih-lu*).[86]

Both of the great private works compiled by Li Hsin-ch'uan rely heavily on government materials. Most of these official histories existed in multiple copies and do not serve to pinpoint his use of the Imperial Library collection except for the daily record.[87] This document appears to have existed in a single copy in the Imperial Archives collection, which makes it probable that he used not only the Imperial Library, but the more secreted Imperial Archives collection where the "daily record" was kept. He does not seem to have been granted permission by the emperor to use the collection, but perhaps only the approval of the Director of the Imperial Library was necessary.

Other noted Southern Sung scholars served in the scholarly agencies and would have had access to the Imperial Library collections. Li Tao, author of the formidable *Hsü Tzu-chih t'ung-chien ch'ang-pien*, served as director and vice-director of the Imperial Library as well as in several positions in the other scholarly agencies.[88] Yüan Shu, who initiated the topical records (*chi-shih pen-mo*) form of history-writing

[82] *NSKKL*(2) 3/2a–2b. *NSKKL*(1) 3/1a and *SHY:CK* 18/27a speak of two directive personnel being in charge of the collections. Perhaps these two sources are speaking of the official chosen daily to supervise the attendants and the official chosen monthly to inspect the collection.

[83] *NSKKL*(1) 3/3a.

[84] *NSKKL*(1) 10/5a.

[85] *NSKKL*(1) 3/2a, 3/1a, *SHY:CK* 18/25b. The Imperial Archives were not to be used in any case. The emperor did borrow from the Imperial Library. See *YH* 26/30–39b. The Court of Imperial Sacrifices and the Imperial Instruction Bureau (*Chiang-yen so*) both were permitted to borrow works from the Imperial Library collections. See *SHY:CK* 18/25b. This, however, appears to be in the period before the rules governing the operation of the Imperial Library were fully established. The latter date probably coincides with the opening of the new Imperial Library building complex in 1144.

[86] *NSKKL*(2) 7/8b, 7/12a, 8/12a, 8/20b, 9/17b, 9/19a, 9/28b.

[87] For the work in which this source is particularly evident see Li Hsin-ch'uan, *Chien-yen i-lai hsi-nien yao-lu* (Shanghai, 1956), 2: pp. 828, 838 *et passim*.

[88] *NSKKL*(1) 7/3a; 7/5b; 8/11b; 8/14a; *NSKKL*(2) 9/9b.

wherein the discussion proceeded by subject rather than in chronological order, served as executive assistant of the Imperial Library, staff author, and assistant staff author as well as compiler in several of the other scholarly agencies.[89]

The Southern Sung bibliophiles from whom we have extant catalogs, Yu Mou, compiler of the *Sui-ch'u t'ang shu-mu* and Ch'ao Kung-wu, compiler of the *Chün-chai tu-shu chih,* served in the scholarly agencies. The former held the positions of executive assistant of the Imperial Library and staff author in addition to other scholarly agency positions,[90] and the latter served as Reign History Bureau compiler (*Kuo-shih yüan pien-hsiu kuan*).[91]

A host of other outstanding Southern Sung scholars might be mentioned who served in the scholarly agencies, including the several who were prominent officials as well. These include Lü Tsu-ch'ien and Chou Pi-ta who were primarily classicists; Wang Ying-lin, author of the *Yü Hai;* Yeh Meng-te, a bibliophile; and the philosopher Chu Hsi, whose influence was to dominate Chinese thought after the thirteenth century.

---

[89] *NSKKL*(2) 7/14b; 8/1a; 9/12b.
[90] *NSKKL*(1) 7/7b; 7/8b; 8/12a; 8/14a; *NSKKL*(2) 9/9b; 9/13a; 9/19b.
[91] *NSKKL*(1) 8/11b.

In all of its aspects, the Imperial Library was a natural product of China's long scholarly tradition and of twelfth-century society and culture. Important as its role in preserving the older literature may have been, two other roles it played were equally important. In a period when the individual activities of the private citizen were assuming a greater place in national life, the Imperial Library provided an agency through which private and governmental scholarship interacted with mutual benefit. In the same period the government was meeting problems far more complex than in earlier times, and assuming greater responsibilities; the Imperial Library played a significant part in its operations, in several ways. It helped to endow these men with the widest fund of knowledge available in that day, and to provide them with more detailed information when it was needed. It was the heart of the state's scholarly activities, giving an element of continuity that other agencies lacked and providing them with staff for their special projects.

The luster of Sung culture and scholarship fascinated the scholarly Chinese imagination during the centuries that were to follow. Much that was best in that intellectual flowering was embodied in the institution of the Imperial Library in its century of renaissance after 1127. It was a worthy symbol of a great era.

APPENDIX

I. THE IMPERIAL LIBRARY BUILDING COMPLEX

Ch'en K'uei provides us with an uncommonly detailed description of the Imperial Library building complex in the *Nan Sung kuan-ko lu*.[1] Since he compiled the work as director of the Imperial Library, one may be assured of its essential accuracy. In the description of the building complex each structure is identified and described along with its furnishings and landscaping. The description is presented in an orderly fashion beginning with the main gate and proceeding on as though one were being given a comprehensive tour of the buildings and grounds. There are only a few exact measurements in the description, several of which concern the walls surrounding the complex. The Imperial Library enclosure was 1,000 feet in length (north to south) and 190 feet in breadth (east to west)[2] while the Reign History Bureau enclosure was perhaps 200 feet in length (north to south) and 160 feet in breadth (east to west). Thus the Imperial Library building complex was laid out in a narrow rectangle on a north–south axis with the Reign History Bureau annex jutting out on its lower southeast side.

Within these walls the buildings were arranged symmetrically and grouped into functional units as described in Chapter II. There are, however, several general problems of interpretation. In the description there are no indications of the distance between buildings; rather in each case we are given the relative position of the structure to be described to the one described last. As the dimensions of the wall are given we have an area of exact shape and dimensions in which to place the whole complex of buildings, a considerable aid in reconstituting them.

Another general problem in reconstituting the layout centers on the absence of any exact dimensions of the buildings. The Imperial Archives is specifically described as a two-story building forty feet high.[3] The shapes of the remaining buildings are not described so exactly. They are, undoubtedly, one story buildings, perhaps twenty to thirty feet in height. The floor areas of buildings are not stated. Instead we are given the number of modules (*chien*), that is the space between four posts, along the front of each structure. Buildings were constructed with rows of posts approximately equidistant from each other. On occasion a post or row of posts would be omitted for certain purposes. One writer gives figures for buildings extant from the Sung period in which modules are approximately sixteen feet square.[4] This is compatible with the data on the Imperial Library buildings and forms the basis for estimating the size of the wall surrounding the Reign History Bureau. A contemporary floor plan would show the location of these posts. One could then count the modules and estimate its size; however, in describing buildings writers often gave only the numbers along the front. Apparently this information and the name of the type of building was enough for the Sung reader to conjure up an image of the structure.[5]

Several other problems of interpretation also need discussion. The first of these is the position of the side gates and their adjacent buildings. It is not clear whether these gates are in the south wall of the Imperial Library building complex to the east and west of the main gate or at the south ends of the east and west walls as they are drawn on the plans prepared for this work. Inasmuch as they are literally termed "side gates" (*p'ien-men*) and no provision is made for them in the otherwise detailed description of the south wall of the complex the latter alternative is chosen.[6] The location of the side gates would probably be less a dilemma if we knew the solution to another problem, that is, the exact shape of the wall surrounding the buildings within. On the plans provided with this study the walls have been drawn straight, but there might have been some irregularities in them. Yet simple jogs in the walls would probably make little difference in the layout of the buildings and significant ones would probably have been mentioned as in the case of the Reign History Bureau.

Another problem arises from apparent textual errors in the *Nan Sung kuan-ko lu* on the number of modules in the east and west lateral buildings (*lang*). According to the text the eastern lateral building has forty-two modules, but an appended note says there are thirty-five.[7] By actual count of those described there are only thirty-three.[8] The western lateral building is said to contain forty-three modules,[9] but those described number only forty-one.[10] Perhaps in each lateral building there were two modules which protruded

---

[1] *NSKKL*(1) 2/1a–8a. This description is supplemented by data in the following sources: *LAC*(1) 1/3b–4a; *LAC*(2) 7/1a–1b; *LAC*(3) 7/1a–22a; Wu Tzu-mu, *Meng-liang lu* (in: *Wu-lin ch'ang-ku ts'ung-pien*), 9/3b–4b.

[2] *NSKKL*(1) 2/1b–2a.

[3] *NSKKL*(1) 2/2a–2b.

[4] Laurence Sickman and Alexander Soper, *The Art and Architecture of China*, pp. 264, 277, and 278.

[5] Li Chieh, *Ying-tsao fa-shih*, 31/2a–2b gives floor plans which show the positioning of posts in typical buildings.

[6] *NSKKL*(1) 2/2a.

[7] *NSKKL*(1) 2/3a.

[8] *NSKKL*(1) 2/3a–4a.

[9] *NSKKL*(1) 2/4a.

[10] *NSKKL*(1) 2/4a–5a.

east and west, rather than forming part of the length of the two structures. If two modules are added to each one they total thirty-five and forty-three, respectively, as is stated in the text; however, there is no specific evidence to corroborate this conjecture. A final problem is inherent in the arrangement of the Compilation Hall and adjacent buildings.[11] The position of the Compilation Hall is somewhat less clear, but in view of the symmetry of the layout, its location as shown appears to be correct.

[11] NSKKL(1) 2/5a–5b.

With these observations in mind one may turn to the "Artists Conception of the Imperial Library Complex" (fig. 7). This is based on Ch'en K'uel's description and the study of numerous graphics from the Sung. It is intended to convey as accurate a picture as possible of the physical surroundings in which scholarly agency personnel worked. The "Detailed Plan of the Imperial Library Building Complex" (fig. 8) is intended for the specialist. Each activity is identified with Chinese characters.

II. IMPERIAL LIBRARY WAGE SCHEDULES AND PERSONNEL DATA

TABLE 8
Directive Personnel Wage Schedule[a]

Position	Basic monthly[b] cash wage			Additional monthly cash allowance for		Total monthly[c] cash wage			Monthly[f] allowance of		Personal staff[g]			
	hsing	shou	shih	Meals[e]	Cash[d]	hsing	shou	shih	Rice	Wheat	Steward	Servant	Courier	Total
Director of the Imperial Library	42	38	35	12	10	64	60	57	10	10	1	6	3	10
Vice-director of the Imperial Library	32	30	28	12	—	44	42	40	7.5	7.5	1	4	2	7
Executive assistant of the Imperial Library	25	22	20	9	—	34	31	29	3	—	1	1	1	3
Staff author	25	22	20	9	—	34	31	29	3	—	1	1	1	3
Librarian of the Imperial Library	22	20	18	9	—	31	29	27	3	—	1	1	1	3
Assistant staff author	22	20	18	9	—	31	29	27	3	—	1	1	1	3
Collator of the Imperial Library	18	16	14	9	—	27	25	23	3	—	1	—	1	3
Correcting editor of the Imperial Library	16	15	14	9	—	25	24	23	3	—	1	—	1	2

[a] Data drawn from NSKKL(1) 9/1a–2b. All cash wage and cash allowance figures are for strings of cash, units of 1,000 copper cash each.

[b] The basic monthly cash wage varied according to the rank of the official filling the position. An official whose rank was too high for the position (hsing) was given a higher cash wage than the official whose rank was appropriate for the position (shou). An official whose rank was too low for the position (shih) was given less yet.

[c] The meal allowance (ch'u-shih-ch'ien) covered the cost of food prepared in the Imperial Library kitchen located west of the Tao Shan Assembly Hall. See Appendix I, fig. 8 "Detailed Plan of the Imperial Library Building Complex."

[d] The additional cash allowance (t'ien-kei-ch'ien), given only to the director of the Imperial Library, appears to have been an additional sum paid for no other reason than that he held this position.

[e] Personnel engaged in official history compilation received an additional cash allowance. Imperial Library directive personnel, according to a proclamation issued in 1139 were to receive an additional monthly tea and soup allowance (ch'a-t'ang-ch'ien) of twenty strings of cash. Another proclamation issued in 1134 provides the following allowances for compilers:
 i. operative personnel received a meal from the kitchen;
 ii. directive personnel in the first category, among others the Compilation director of the National History (Chien-hsiu kuo-shih), received forty strings of cash;
 iii. directive personnel in the second category, that is the official in charge of the Imperial Library and his assistant, received thirty-seven and one-half strings of cash;
 iv. directive personnel in the third category, that is the remainder of the Imperial Library directive personnel from staff author to correcting editor of the Imperial Library, received thirty-five strings of cash.

[f] Rice and wheat figures are for piculs (shih), .55 U. S. bushels. This and other such figures are drawn from Wu Ch'eng-lo, Chung-kuo tu-liang-heng shih (Shanghai, 1937).

[g] The figures given for the number on the personal staff of directive personnel serving in the Imperial Library are according to the new law as stated in NSKKL(1) 9/2a–2b. The old law referred to in the same source is apparently the one recorded in LTKS 4/14a and dated 1114. Thus, the new law is later than 1114, probably early Southern Sung.

In addition to cash, grain, and a personal staff, directive personnel serving in the Imperial Library were given garments in the spring and winter. The quantity and quality of the garments were appropriate to their rank. Men of certain ranks were given cloth instead of one of the garments in the winter. In the spring, the director and vice-director of the Imperial Library received an outer garment for public use (lo-kung-fu), an undershirt (han-shan), and a pair of lined underpants (chia-k'u). The number and kinds of items provided in the winter were the same, except that they were made of a different cloth and in the case of the outer garment for public use, lined. The remaining personnel received fewer of these items and usually they were made of a different quality material; however, everyone received an outer garment for public use.

TABLE 9

OPERATIVE PERSONNEL WAGE SCHEDULE[a]

Billet	Basic monthly[b] cash wage		Additional monthly cash allowance for			Total monthly cash wage	Monthly allowance[f] of		Annual allowance[g] of	
	Food	Other	Meals[c]	Family support[d]	Wheat[e]		Rice	Wheat	Silk cloth	Cotton wadding
Tu-k'ung-mu kuan	8.5	8.5	9	4.5	3	33.50	1.5	1.5	20	20
K'ung-mu kuan	7.5	7.5	9	4.5	3	31.50	1	1	10	15
Ssu-k'u shu-chih kuan	5	5	9	4.5	2	25.50	1	1	44	10
Shu-chih kuan	5	5	9	4.5	2	25.50	1	1	4	10
Piao-tsou kuan	4.5	4.5	9	4.5	2	22.50	1	—	4	10
Shu-k'u kuan	4	4	9	3.5	—	20.50	1	—	4	10
Shou-tang kuan	4	4	9	3.5	—	20.50	1	—	4	10
Cheng-ming k'ai-shu	3	5	7.2	2.25	—	17.45	2	—	—	—
Shou-ch'üeh	3	3.5	7.2	2.25	—	15.95	—	—	—	—
Cheng-hsi-ming	4	—	7.2	2.25	—	15.45	—	—	—	—
Shou-ch'üeh hsi-ming	3	—	7.2	2.25	—	12.45	—	—	—	—
T'ou-ming-jen	—	—	—	—	—	—	—	—	—	—

[a] Data drawn from *NSKKL*(1) 9/1a–2b. All cash wages and cash allowances are for strings of cash. See table 3 for a translation of these titles and note a of the same table for a discussion of them.

[b] The basic monthly cash wage in this case is made up of two parts, food (*t'ien-kei shih-ch'ien*) and an additional allowance for other items (*liao-ch'ien*). However, it should be noted that the food allowance is given in each case; whereas the additional allowance is given in nine of the eleven cases.

[c] The monthly meal allowance is actually a Daily Meal Allowance (*jih-chih shih-ch'ien*). It was set at .3 string of cash a day.

[d] The family support allowance (*shan-chia-ch'ien*).

[e] The wheat allowance (*mai-ch'e-ch'ien*).

[f] Rice and wheat figures are for piculs (*shih*), .55 U. S. bushel.

[g] Silk cloth (*i-chüan*) was issued in equal amounts in spring and winter. Figures are for *p'i*, a measure of 8.1 square yards. Cotton wadding (*mien*) was issued in winter only. Figures are for taels (*liang*), 1.3 ounces.

Tables 8, 9, and 10 suggest the relative standing of the three groups which made up the Imperial Library staff (see fig. 5). Directive personnel, in general, stood only a bit higher than the operative personnel. The proximate standing of these two groups to each other is further evidenced when their wage schedules

TABLE 10

WAGE SCHEDULE OF THE PERSONAL STAFF OF THE DIRECTIVE PERSONNEL

Personal staff[a]	Basic monthly[b] cash wage	Monthly[c] cash meal allowance	Monthly[d] commuted cash allowance	Total monthly cash wage	Monthly[e] rice allowance	Annual[f] silk cloth allowance	Annual[g] cotton cloth allowance	Annual[h] allowance of cotton wadding
Steward	2	5.4	.72	8.12	.54	—	—	—
Servant	1.5	5.4	.72	7.62	.54	2	1	10
Courier	1.8	5.4	.72	7.92	.54	—	—	—

[a] The data presented in the accompanying table are drawn from a text and an adjacent footnote in *NSKKL*(1) 9/2a–2b. It gives the number of personal staff members budgeted for each of the directive personnel on duty in the Imperial Library and their salaries. Unfortunately, the text and the footnote are both devoid of additional information. No further data could be found to augment this information or corroborate what might be implied from the literal meaning of their titles. Therefore, the translations of personal staff titles and the statements on their duties are tentative suggestions.

i. Steward. *T'ing-tzu.* Duty: household manager. Each official had a steward regardless of rank. That he is the highest paid of the three types of personal staff members suggests a position of authority.

ii. Servant. *I-liang ch'in-shih kuan.* Duty: household servant. A literal reading of the characters in the title strongly suggests the varied functions of a servant. The variable number and low salary may be additional corroborative evidence.

iii. Courier. *Ch'eng-sung.* Duty: conduct of affairs outside the household. The characters in the title connote the function of courier. Again, the variable number and medium salary may be additional corroborative evidence.

[b] Basic monthly cash wage (*liao-ch'ien*). All cash wage and cash allowance figures are for strings of cash.

[c] Monthly cash meal allowance (*mei-jih shih-ch'ien*) is actually a daily cash allowance of 18 strings of cash a day.

[d] Monthly commuted cash allowance (*kei-ch'e mai-ch'ien*).

[e] Figures are for piculs (*shih*), .55 U. S. bushel.

[f] Annual silk cloth allowance (*i-chüan*) was issued in equal shares in spring and winter. Figures are for *p'i*, a measure of 8.1 square yards.

[g] Annual cotton cloth allowance (*pu*) was issued in the spring. Figures are for *p'i*, a measure of 8.1 square yards.

[h] Annual allowance of cotton wadding (*mien*) was issued in the winter. Figures are for taels (*liang*), 1.3 ounces.

TABLE 11

CIVIL SERVICE EXAMINATION STANDING AND GROUP (*Chia*) DISTRIBUTION

Examination standing	Group (*chia*)	All successful examinees				Imperial Library[c] directive personnel 1131–1190	
		1148 list[a]		1256 list[b]			
		No.	%	No.	%	No.	%
Passed with distinction	1	29	9	61	10.6	113	37.4
	2						
Formally qualified	3	37	11	79	12.7	125	41.4
Passed	4	264	80	461	76.7	64	21.2
	5						
Totals		330	100	601	100.0	302	100.0

[a] Data drawn from Hsü Nai-ch'ang, *Sung Yüan k'o-chü san-lu* (1923).
[b] *Ibid.*
[c] Data drawn from *NSKKL*(1) 7/1a–13B, 8/1a–14b; *NSKKL*(2) 7/1a–22a, 8/1a–28b, 9/1a–29b.

are compared to the "Wage Schedule of the Personal Staff of the Directive Personnel" (see table 10). This group, roughly approximating the service personnel, is distinctly lower than both the directive and operative personnel.

The wage schedules are only one indicator of the relative standing of the three groups. While they are useful in this regard it should be borne in mind that the directive personnel as members of the civil service could supplement their official cash income by participating in document compilation and history-writing projects. Moreover, they probably enjoyed a social standing out of proportion to their salary and more in keeping with their role as the leaders in society. This is clearly indicated by the personal staff with which they were provided and the distinctive clothing they were given also. Wages then are not a clear indicator of social standing, but they do suggest the relative standing of three groups of government employees in Southern Sung society.

Civil service examination data provide us with an insight into the career patterns of directive personnel. Table 11 displays the standing of those who passed the examination in 1148 and 1256. These are the only two lists extant from the Southern Sung. The successful examinees were ranked in order of achievement and then placed into groups (*chia*). Those who stood at the head of the list were honored with the distinction of having all others on it referred to as being examinees on his list. Table 12 lists all civil service examination laureates, that is those who placed first, for the period 1131–1190.

Tables 13, 14, and 15 give a number of insights into the career patterns of Southern Sung directive personnel as indicated by their tour, or in some cases

tours, of duty in the Imperial Library. It is possible to study the actual number of directive personnel on duty in the Imperial Library in table 13 with one qualification and that is, that it indicates the maximum number on duty in any single year in the period 1131–1190. This necessary expedient was followed to reduce the data to order. On occasion one position may have been occupied by two or more persons in one year. Table 13 is graphically displayed in fig. 6 which precedes it. The rise and fall in the number of personnel on duty changed markedly at times. This and other features of Imperial Library directive personnel are dealt with in chapter III. See also tables 2, 3 and 4.

Some indication of the previous career of those directive personnel assigned to the Imperial Library may be gleaned from table 14. In addition we have given data on the length of time that personnel served in their initial appointment to the Imperial Library in this table. The results would be of greater interest

TABLE 12

CIVIL SERVICE EXAMINATION LAUREATES, 1131–1190[a]

Year	Civil Service examination laureate	Total no. passed
1132	Chang Chiu-ch'eng	379[b]
1135	Wang Ying-ch'en	357[b]
1138	Huang Kung-tu	293[b]
1142	Ch'en Ch'eng-chih	398[b]
1145	Liu Chang	373[b]
1148	Wang Tso	353[b]
1151	Chao K'uei	422[b]
1154	Chang Hsiao-hsiang	411[b]
1157	Wang Shih-p'eng	426
1160	Liang K'e-chia	428[b]
1163	Mu Tai-wen	541
1166	Hsiao Kuo-liang	492
1169	Cheng Ch'iao	592
1172	Huang Ting	389
1175	Chan K'uei	426
1178	Yao Ying	417
1181	Huang Yu	379
1184	Wei Ching	395
1187	Wang Jung	435
1190	Yü Hsia	557

[a] Those who passed the triennial civil service examination were listed in order of accomplishment. The men who headed each list were designated examination laureates. Thereafter the list bore their names. When one wanted to cite the year in which a man passed the civil service examination, the name of the examination laureate was used rather than the actual year. By dating the examination laureates for each triennial examination, it has been possible to give the civil service examination year for the successful examinees for almost all directive personnel who served in the Imperial Library from 1131 to 1190. The data in this list are drawn from *TK* 32/32b–34a. See Edward A. Kracke, Jr., *Civil Service in Early Sung China*, pp. 58–72 for a description of the Northern Sung civil service recruitment examination system.

[b] This figure includes those who passed the civil service examination from Szechwan who were examined locally because of the distance to the capital and the difficulty of travel in the first few decades of the Southern Sung.

TABLE 13

MAXIMUM NUMBER OF DIRECTIVE PERSONNEL, APPOINTMENTS ANNUALLY, 1131–1190[a]

Position	1131	1132	1133	1134	1135	1136	1137	1138	1139	1140	1141	1142	1143	1144	1145	1146	1147	1148	1149	1150	1151	1152	1153	1154	1155	1156	1157	1158	1159	1160
Director of the Imperial Library	—	—	—	—	—	—	—	—	—	—	—	—	—	—	—	—	—	—	—	—	—	—	—	—	—	—	—	—	—	—
Vice-director of the Imperial Library	—	1	1	1	—	—	—	—	1	1	—	1	1	1	—	—	—	—	—	1	1	1	—	—	1	1	1	—	1	1
Executive assistant of the Imperial Library	1	1	1	1	1	1	1	1	1	1	—	1	1	1	1	—	—	—	1	1	1	1	—	—	1	1	1	2	1	1
Staff author	1	—	1	—	—	1	2	2	—	—	1	2	1	2	2	2	—	—	—	—	—	—	—	—	1	—	—	2	2	—
Librarian of the Imperial Library	—	1	1	1	1	1	2	2	2	2	2	2	2	1	1	—	1	1	1	1	1	1	1	1	1	2	2	2	1	1
Assistant staff author	—	—	1	1	2	2	2	2	2	2	2	—	2	2	2	2	1	1	2	1	1	1	1	—	1	2	2	2	—	1
Collator of the Imperial Library	2	—	—	2	1	—	3	3	4	4	2	10	2	1	1	3	1	1	2	—	3	2	2	—	1	2	6	4	5	3
Correcting editor of the Imperial Library	1	2	1	4	9	12	8	6	8	7	7	2	5	3	3	3	2	2	1	—	—	1	1	1	2	4	2	5	4	3
Total	5	5	5	10	15	19	17	17	18	17	14	17	14	9	10	5	4	4	5	4	5	5	4	2	7	10	13	16	14	10

Position	1161	1162	1163	1164	1165	1166	1167	1168	1169	1170	1171	1172	1173	1174	1175	1176	1177	1178	1179	1180	1181	1182	1183	1184	1185	1186	1187	1188	1189	1190
Director of the Imperial Library	—	—	—	—	—	—	—	—	—	—	—	—	—	—	—	—	—	—	—	—	—	—	—	—	—	—	—	—	—	—
Vice-director of the Imperial Library	—	1	—	1	1	—	1	—	—	—	—	—	—	—	1	1	1	1	—	1	1	—	1	1	1	1	1	1	—	1
Executive assistant of the Imperial Library	1	1	1	1	1	1	1	1	1	1	1	—	1	—	1	—	1	1	1	1	1	—	1	1	1	—	—	1	—	—
Staff author	—	—	—	—	—	—	—	—	—	—	1	1	1	1	2	2	2	2	2	2	1	1	1	2	2	2	2	1	1	1
Librarian of the Imperial Library	—	2	1	2	2	2	1	2	2	2	1	1	2	1	2	2	2	2	2	2	2	2	1	2	2	2	2	2	2	2
Assistant staff author	1	2	2	2	2	2	1	2	2	2	2	2	2	2	2	2	2	2	1	2	1	2	1	1	2	2	2	1	2	2
Collator of the Imperial Library	1	2	3	3	4	3	2	—	3	3	3	3	1	3	3	4	5	3	2	4	5	3	2	3	2	1	1	1	1	1
Correcting editor of the Imperial Library	4	5	7	3	2	4	5	5	5	4	3	2	6	6	3	1	1	2	3	2	1	3	1	3	2	—	1	1	2	1
Total	8	11	12	10	11	12	10	9	12	15	13	11	15	13	15	13	14	14	12	14	13	10	9	9	10	9	10	10	10	10

[a] Data drawn from *NSKKL*(1) 7/1a–13b, 8/1a–14b; *NSKKL*(2) 7/1a–22a, 8/1a–28b, 9/1a–29b. These appear to be the personnel records for the directive personnel who served in the Imperial Library. One man did not replace another on the day he left. A month or more might elapse before a replacement arrived; hence table 13 indicates the maximum number of personnel on duty for each position annually.

TABLE 14

Previous Career and Tenure of Directive
Personnel, 1131–1190[a]

Group	Time span from civil service examination to initial appointment	Average tenure of initial appointment
Imperial Library[b] Directive Personnel	18.9 years	25.3 months
Sub-group		
Civil service[c] examination laureates	3.1 years	33.6 montns
Chief councilors[d]	9.1 years	21.6 months
Assisting councilors[e]	12.1 years	20.6 months

[a] Data drawn from *NSKKL*(1) 7/1a–13b, 8/1a–14b; *NSKKL*(2) 7/1a–22a, 8/1a–28b, 9/1a–29b.

[b] Of the 302 persons on duty in the Imperial Library from 1131 to 1190 who passed the civil service examination in the regular manner, the examination dates for 290 could be determined. See table 12, note "a" for the means of arriving at civil service examination dates.

[c] All civil service examination laureates in the period 1131 to 1190 later served in the Imperial Library.

[d] The total number of officials who would later serve as chief councilors for the period 1131–1190 was twenty-three, nine of whom served in the Imperial Library.

[e] The total number of officials who would later serve as assisting councilors for the period 1131–1190 was ninety-nine, thirty of whom had served in the Imperial Library.

if they could be compared with other agencies of the government.

TABLE 15

Directive Personnel Experience in Imperial
Library Positions, 1131–1190[a]

Position	Number who held the position	Per cent who served previously
Director of the Imperial Library	7	100
Vice-director of the Imperial Library	54	50
Executive assistant of the Imperial Library	53	15
Staff author	48	85
Librarian of the Imperial Library	70	36
Assistant staff author	81	78
Collator of the Imperial Library	—[b]	—
Correcting editor of the Imperial Library	—	—

[a] Data drawn from *NSKKL*(1) 7/1a–13b, 8/1a–14b; *NSKKL*(2) 7/1a–22a, 8/1a–28b, 9/1a–29b.

[b] Virtually all collators and correcting editors of the Imperial Library held these positions as their initial appointments; thus no figures have been given for them.

Finally table 15 displays the results of a study of experience within the Imperial Library directive personnel ranks. It is of interest that most personnel were assigned with experience in the Imperial Library except for the two lowest positions. A final note on table 15, the small number of persons who held the position of director of the Imperial Library is a result of there being few assigned rather than because of long tenure of office.

III. LIST OF CHINESE CHARACTERS

A-ku-ta 阿古打

an 案

An Lu-shan 安祿山

cha 札

ch'a-t'ang-ch'ien 茶湯錢

Chang K'uei 詹騤

Chang Chiu-ch'eng 張九成

Chang Hsiao-hsiang 張孝祥

Chang Lun 張掄

Chang Mou 張楙

Chao I-fu 趙以夫

Chao K'uei 趙逵

chao-shih 召試

Chao T'ing 趙挺

Chao Wen Kuan 昭文館

Ch'ao Kung-wu 晁公武

Che Tsung 哲宗

Chen Tsung 真宗

Ch'en Ch'eng-chih 陳誠之

Ch'en Yang 陳暘

Cheng Ch'iao 鄭僑

Cheng-ho ch'ung-hsiu kuo-ch'ao
　　hui-yao 政和重修國朝會要

Cheng-hsi-ming 正係名

Cheng-ming k'ai-shu 正名楷書

cheng-shih 正史

Cheng T'ing 正廳

ch'eng 丞

Ch'eng-sung 承送

Chi Hsien Tien 集賢殿

Chi Hsien Tien Shu-yüan 集賢殿書院

chi-shih pen-mo 記事本末

chi-ti 及第

ch'i-chü chu 起居注

chia 甲

chia-k'u 夾袴

Chiang-yen so 講筵所

chien (module) 間

chien (industrial prefecture) 監

Chien 監

Chien-hsiu kuo-shih 監修國史

Chien-k'ang 建康

Chien k'u-tzu 監庫子

chien-ssu 監司

ch'ien 錢

chih (administrator) 知

chih (monograph) 志

Chih chao-wen kuan 直昭文館

Chih-cheng 執政

chih-hsien 知縣

Chih-hsüeh shih 直學士

Chih-tsa an 知雜案

chin-shih 進士

Ch'in Hsi 秦熺

Ch'in Tsung 欽宗

Ching-chi an 經籍案

Ching-chiang 靜江

Ch'ing Ho Fang 清河坊

Ch'iu-shu ch'üeh-chi 求書關記

chou (roll) 軸

chou (prefecture) 州

Chou i 周易

Chou wen-hsüeh 州文學

Chu-pan an 祝版案

chu-pu 主簿

Chu-tso lang 著作郎

Chu-tso shu-mu 著作書目

Chu Tso T'ing 著作庭

Chu-tso tso-lang 著作佐郎

ch'u-shen 出身

ch'u-shih-ch'ien 廚食錢

chüan 卷

Ch'üan-chou 泉州

chuang-yüan 狀元

chün 單

Ch'un-ch'iu 春秋

Chung-hsing kuan-ko shu-mu 中興館閣書目

Chung-ku yüan 鐘鼓院

Chung-shu men-hsia 中書門下

Chung-shu sheng 中書省

Ch'ung Wen Yüan 崇文院

Erh-fu chung-i 二府忠義

Fa Hui Ssu 法惠寺

fu 府

Fu-cnou 富州

Fu Wen Ko 敷文閣

Han Ch'i 韓琦

han-shan 汗衫

Han shu 漢書

Han-tan shu-chih 邯鄲書志

Han Yü 韓愈

Hang-chou 杭州

Ho K'e-chung 何克忠

Ho Lin 賀廩

Hsi hu 西湖

Hsi Kuan 西館

Hsiao ching 孝經

Hsiao Kuo-liang	蕭國梁	hui-yao	會要
Hsiao Tsung	孝宗	Hui-yao so	會要所
hsien	縣	Hui Yu Ko	徽猷閣
Hsien Mu Ko	顯謨閣	Hung Hsi	洪羲
Hsien Wen Ko	顯文閣	I-chieh	易解
Hsien-yang	咸陽	I ching	易經
hsing	行	i-chüan	衣絹
Hsing-chu kuan	行主管	I-liang ch'in-shih kuan	衣糧親事官
Hsing-pu	刑部	Jen Tsung	仁宗
Hsiu kuo-shih	修國史	Jen Tsung huang-ti shih-lu	仁宗皇帝實錄
Hsiung-nu	匈奴	jih-chih shih-ch'ien	日支食錢
Hsü Chung	許中	jih-li	日曆
hsüan-lun sheng-yü	宣諭聖語	Jih-li so	日曆所
Hsüeh-shih	學士	K'ai-feng	開封
Hsüeh-shih yüan	學士院	Kao Tsung	高宗
Hu-chou	湖州	kei-ch'e mai-ch'ien	給折麥錢
Hu-pu	戶部	K'u-tzu	庫子
Hua Wen Ko	華文閣	kuan	貫
Huai Ch'ing Fang	懷慶坊	Kuang Tsung	光宗
Huan Chang Ko	煥章閣	Kung-pu	工部
Huang Ch'ao	黃巢	Kung-shih-k'u	公使庫
Huang Kung-tu	黃公度	Kung-Sun Hung	公孫弘
Huang Meng	黃濛	Kung Tsung	恭宗
Huang Ting	黃定	K'ung-mu kuan	孔目官
Huang Yu	黃由	Kuo-ch'ao hui-yao	國朝會要
Hui Tsung	惠施	Kuo-ch'ao hui-yao tsung-lei	國朝會要總類

Kuo-ch'ao pao-hsün 國朝寶訓

kuo-shih 國史

Kuo-shih jih-li so 國史日曆所

Kuo-shih yüan 國史院

Kuo-shih yüan pien-hsiu kuan 國史院編修官

Kuo-tzu chien 國子監

lang 廊

Lao-tzu 老子

Li Chi 禮記

Li-pu (personnel) 吏部

Li-pu (rites) 禮部

Li Shih-min 李世民

Li Shou-chih 李授之

Li Shu 李淑

Li Tsung 理宗

liang 兩

Liang-che-hsi 兩浙西

Liang-che-tung 兩浙東

Liang K'e-chia 梁克家

liao-ch'ien 料錢

lieh-chuan 列傳

Lin Shu 林攄

Lin Yen 林儀

Liu Chang 劉章

Liu-ch'ao hui-yao 六朝會要

Liu-ch'ao kuo-shih chih 六朝國史志

Liu hsiang 劉向

Liu hsin 劉歆

Liu Pang 劉邦

lo-kung-fu 羅公服

lu 錄

Lü Tsu-ch'ien 呂祖謙

Lung T'u Ko 龍圖閣

Lung-t'u ko hsüeh-shih 龍圖閣學士

mai-ch'e-ch'ien 麥折錢

Mao 毛

mei-jih shih-ch'ien 每日食錢

Men-hsia sheng 門下省

Meng-tzu 孟子

mien 緜

Ming-ch'en lieh-chuan 名臣列傳

mu-chih 慕職

Mu Tai-wen 朱待問

Nan-ching 南京

Nan Sung kuan-ko lu 南宋館閣錄

Ning Tsung 寧宗

Ou-yang Hsiu 歐陽修

pan 板

Pan Ku 班固

Pao Chang Ko 寶章閣

pao-hsün 寶訓

Pao Mu Ko 寶謨閣

Pao Wen Ko 寶文閣

Pi Ko 秘閣

Pi-ko chu-k'u shu-mu 秘閣諸庫書目

Pi-shu ch'eng 秘書丞

Pi-shu chien 秘書監

Pi-shu lang 秘書郎

Pi-shu shao-chien 秘書少監

Pi-shu sheng 秘書省

Pi-shu sheng cheng-tzu 秘書省正字

Pi-shu sheng chiao-shu lang 秘書省校書郎

Pi-shu tsung-mu 秘書總目

p'i 疋

Piao-tsou kuan 表奏官

Pieh lu 別錄

Pien-hsiu hui-yao so 編修會要所

Pien-hsiu kuan 編修官

p'ien-men 偏門

Ping-pu 兵部

P'ing-chiang 平江

Pu 補

pu 布

Pu-hsieh so 補寫所

San-ch'ao kuo-shih 三朝國史

San-ssu 三司

shan-chia-ch'ien 贍家錢

Shang-shu sheng 尚書省

Shao-hsing 紹興

Shen Tsung 神宗

Shen Tsung huang-ti shih-lu 神宗皇帝實錄

sheng-cheng 聖政

sheng-kuan 省貫

shih (wage) 試

shih (piculs) 石

shih-cheng chi 時政記

Shih chi 史記

Shih ching 詩經

Shih Ch'ü Ko 石渠閣

Shih Kuan 史館

shih-lu 實錄

Shih-lu yüan 實錄院

shou 守

Shou-ch'üeh 守闕

Shou-ch'üeh hsi-ming 守闕係名

Shou-tang kuan 守當官

shu 書

Shu-chih kuan 書直官

Shu ching 書經

Shu-hsieh k'ai-shu 書寫楷書

Shu-k'u kuan 書庫官

Shu-mi yüan 樞密院

sou-fang 搜訪

sou-fang k'u 搜訪庫

Ssu-ch'ao kuo-shih shih-lu 四朝國史實錄

Ssu-k'u shu chih kuan 四庫書直官

Ssu-Ma Ch'ien 司馬遷

Ssu-Ma Kuang 司馬光

ssu-pu 四部

Ta-nei 大內

Ta Sung shih-kuan shu-mu 大宋史館書目

Tai-chih 待制

T'ai-ch'ing shao-ching 太常少卿

T'ai-ch'ang ssu 太常寺

T'ai Ch'ing Lou 太清樓

T'ai Ch'ing Lou shu-mu 太清樓書目

T'ai-shang huang-ti sheng-cheng 太上皇帝聖政

T'ai-shih an 太史案

T'ai-shih chü 太史局

T'ai Tsu 太祖

T'ai Tsu huang-ti shih-lu 太祖皇帝實錄

T'ai Tsung 太宗

T'ai Tsung huang-ti shih-lu 太宗皇帝實錄

T'ai Tsung huang-ti yü-shu 太宗皇帝御書

T'ang (Reign History Hall) 唐

T'ang K'ai 唐開

tao (sheets) 道

Tao Shan T'ang 道山堂

t'e-t'zu chin-shih 特賜進士

ti-chi 帝記

Ti Ping 帝昺

T'i-chü Kuo-shih yüan 提舉國史院

T'i-chü Pi-shu sheng 提舉祕書省

T'i Chü So Shu-k'u 提舉所書庫

T'i Chü T'ing Chia Men 提舉廳夾門

Tien-chien wen-tzu 點檢文字

T'ien Chang Ko 天章閣

T'ien-chang ko tai-chih 天章閣待制

T'ien Ching Fang 天井坊

T'ien Hao 田鎬

t'ien-kei-ch'ien 添給錢

t'ien-kei shih-ch'ien 添給食錢

T'ien-sheng nan-chiao lu-pu ts'e-chi 天聖南交鹵簿冊記

T'ien-shih shu-mu 田氏書目

T'ing-tzu 廳子

T'ou-ming-jen 投名人

Tsai-hsiang 宰相

ts'e 冊

Ts'e-yen hun-i k'o-lou so 測驗渾儀刻漏所

Tseng Min 曾旼

Tseng T'ung 曾統

Tseng Wen-fu 曾溫夫

Tsu Tsung shih-lu 祖宗實錄

Tu-k'ung-mu kuan 都孔目官

tu-tieh 度牒

Tu Tsung 度宗

Tuan Tsung 端宗

T'ung Che Fang 通浙坊

t'ung-ch'u-shen 同出身

T'ung-hsiu kuo-shih 同修國史

t'ung-p'an 通判

t'zu chin-shih 賜進士

Wang Ang 王昂

Wang Jung 王容

Wang Kuei 王珪

Wang Shih-p'eng 王十朋

Wang Tso 王佐

Wang Yao-ch'en 王堯臣

wei 魏

Wei Ching 衛涇

Wei Hsü 韋許

wen-chi 文記

Wen Te Tien 文德殿

Yao Ying 姚穎

Yeh-lü A-pao-chi 耶律阿保機

Yen I 嚴抑

Ying Tsung 英宗

Ying Tsung huang-ti shih-lu 英宗皇帝實錄

Yu Wen Tien 右文殿

Yu Yü 尤婿

yü-cha 御札

Yü Hsia 余復

Yü Shen 余深

Yüan Shu 袁淑

yung-mien wen-chieh 永免文解

BIBLIOGRAPHY

ESSAY ON SOURCES

The sources on which this monograph is based are largely works compiled by the agencies studied, the Imperial Library and the associated scholarly agencies. The most significant collections of data are in two works, one designed to be a sequel to the other, which sum up scholarly agency activities to 1178 and ca. 1270, respectively. These were not unique types of works, for contemporary bibliographies extant today indicate that other agencies of the government prepared summary accounts of their activities on appropriate occasions. The first work by Ch'en K'uei, an official who held a number of positions in the scholarly agencies including that of director of the Imperial Library at the time this work was compiled, is entitled the *Nan Sung kuan-ko lu*. Originally it contained ten chapters, the first of which is lost, but apparently dealt with these agencies in a summary fashion. Chapter two describes the building complex, three the holdings of the Imperial Library, four the compilation work of the associated scholarly agencies, five the literary pieces composed by members of the civil service who served in these agencies, six the notable miscellaneous events which touch on the agencies, seven and eight the personnel records of the agencies, nine the salary schedules for agency personnel, and ten the administrative and personnel regulations which specifically pertain to these agencies. The *Nan Sung kuan-ko hsü-lu* continues the record of the operation of the scholarly agencies in a manner almost identical to the first work. Both works were drawn from the *Yung-lo ta-tien*.

All other sources cover portions of the same ground as these agency accounts, usually in less detail, or in some cases add new material. That complementary source material is available, of course, is a great asset. The most valuable work in this regard is the *Sung hui-yao chi-kao*, a collection of government documents. Its material is arranged by agencies according to the organization of the government and chronologically under each agency. This work touches on every phase of the organization and operation of the scholarly agencies, but usually with less detail than the *Nan Sung kuan-ko lu* and *hsü-lu* mentioned above.

Two well-known encyclopedias, Ma Tuan-lin's *Wen-hsien t'ung-kao* and Wang Ying-lin's *Yü-hai* are quite useful in that their topical arrangement makes it possible to verify a point reliably and quickly. A topical history with similar contents where they touch on the Sung is Li Hsin-ch'uan's *Chien-yen i-lai ch'ao-yeh tsa-chi*. Although limited in scope it does treat the scholarly agencies. Broader in coverage, although a less satisfactory work, is T'o T'o and others, *Sung-shih*. The topical arrangement of these works is usefully complemented by two chronologically arranged works: Li Tao's *Hsü Tzu-chih t'ung-chien* for the Northern Sung and Li Hsin-ch'uan's *Chien-yen i-lai hsi-yen yao-lu* for the Southern Sung.

The description of the scholarly agency building complex may be supplemented by details from Li Chieh's *Ying-tsao fa-shih*, a technical builder's manual; reminiscenses of the capital such as Wu Tzu-mu's *Meng Liang-lu* and the gazetteers extant from the period, but particularly Ch'ien Yüeh-yu's *Hsien-ch'un Lin-an-chih* which contains a number of Southern Sung maps of Hang-chou. It includes one which shows the location of the Imperial Library building complex.

Annotated library catalogs are quite useful also. For the Northern Sung Imperial Library collections there is Wang Yao-chian's *Ch'ung-wen ts'ung-mu* and for the Southern Sung Imperial Library collections there are also catalogs. At the time the *Nan Sung kuan-ko lu* was prepared a companion catalog of the Imperial Library entitled the *Chung-hsing kuan-ko shu-mu* was compiled. In 1220 a similar catalog entitled the *Chung-hsing kuan-ko hsü-shu-mu* was completed. The remnants of these catalogs have been collected by Chao Shih-wei in a work entitled the *Chung-hsing kuan-ko shu-mu chi-k'ao*. Additional useful catalogs are those of private Southern Sung libraries: Ch'en Kung-wu, *Chün-chai tu-shu chih*; Ch'en Chen-sun, *Chih-chai shu-lu chieh-t'i*; Yu Mou, *Sui-ch'u t'ang shu-mu*.

The personnel records of the scholarly agencies in the *Nan Sung kuan-ku lu* and *hsü-lu* are a useful guide to the largest untapped body of Sung source material, the collected papers of scholar-officials (*wen-chi*). A certain amount of official material was found in this type of work. Generally the documents are more complete than those found in other types of works.

LIST OF ABBREVIATIONS

CHSC   Huang Sung Chung-hsing liang-ch'ao sheng-cheng   皇宋中興兩朝聖政

CHWC   Hui-an hsien-sheng Chu-wen kung wen-chi   晦菴先生朱文公文集

CKFC   Chih-kuan fen-chi   職官分紀

CYTC   Chien-yen i-lai ch'ao-yeh tsa-chi   建炎以來朝野雜記

LAC(1)   Ch'ien-tao Lin-an chih   乾道臨安志

LAC(2)   Ch'un-yu Lin-an chih   淳祐臨安志

LAC(3)   Hsien-ch'un Lin-an chih   咸淳臨安志

LTKS   Lin-t'ai ku-shih   麟臺故事

NSKKL(1)   Nan Sung kuan-ko lu   南宋館閣錄

NSKKL(2)   Nan Sung kuan-ko hsü lu   南宋館閣續錄

NSKKSM   Chung-hsing kuan-ko shu-mu chi-k'ao   中興館閣書目輯考

SCSS   Sung-ch'ao shih-shih   宋朝事實

SCT   Sui-ch'u t'ang shu-mu   遂初堂書目

SHY:CJ   Sung hui-yao chi-kao:ch'ung-ju   宋會要輯稿：崇儒

SHY:CK   Sung hui-yao chi-kao:chih-kuan   宋會要輯稿：職官

SHY:FYü   Sung hui-yao chi-kao:fang-yü   宋會要輯稿：方域

SHY:HC   Sung hui-yao chi-kao:hsüan-chü   宋會要輯稿：選舉

SHY:YL   Sung hui-yao chi-kao:yün-li   宋會要輯稿：運歷

SLCT   Chih-chai shu-lu chieh-t'i   直齋書錄解題

SLYY   Shih-lin yen-yü   石林燕語

SPPY   Ssu-pu pei-yao   四部備要

SPTK   Ssu-pu ts'ung-k'an   四部叢刊

SS   Sung shih   宋史

TK   Wen-hsien t'ung-k'ao   文獻通考

YH   Yü hai   玉海

LIST OF BOOKS AND ARTICLES CITED

Bailyn, Bernard. 1960. Education in the Forming of American Society (Chapel Hill).

Ben-David, Joseph. 1971. The Scientist's Role in Society: A Comparative Study (Englewood Cliffs).

Bolgar, R. R. 1964. The Classical Heritage and its Beneficiaries from the Carolingian Age to the End of the Renaissance (New York).

Carter, Thomas F. 1955. The Invention of Printing and its Spread Westward (Rev. ed., New York).

Chao Shih-wei 趙士煒 (comp.). 1933. Chung-hsing kuan-ko shu-mu chi-k'ao 中興館閣書目輯考 (Peking).

Ch'ao Kung-wu 晁公武. 1929. Chün-chai tu-shu chih 郡齋讀書 (Shanghai).

Ch'en Chen-sung 陳振孫. 1883. Chih-chai shu-lu chieh-t'i 直齋書錄解題. (Chiang-su).

Ch'en, Kenneth K. S. 1964. Buddhism in China: An Historical Survey (Princeton).

Ch'en K'uei 陳騤. 1886. Nan Sung kuan-ko lu 南宋館閣錄. In Wu-lin ch'ang-ku ts'ung-pien 武林掌故叢編.

Ch'eng Chü 程俱. 1879. Lin-t'ai ku-shih 麟臺故事. In Shih-wan-chüan lou ts'ung-shu 十萬卷樓叢書.

Ch'ien Yüeh-yu 潛說友. 1830. Hsien-ch'un Lin-an chih 咸淳臨安志.

Ching-k'ang yao-lu 靖康安錄. 1830. In Shih-wan chüan lou ts'ung-shu 十萬卷樓叢書.

Chou Pi-ta 周必大. 1876. Yü-t'ang lei-hui 玉堂類彙. In Chou-i kuo-wen chung-kung chi 周益國文忠公集.

Chou Tsung 周淙. 1886. Ch'ien-tao Lin-an chih 乾道臨安志. In Wu-lin
　　　ch'amg-ku ts'ung-pien 武林掌故叢編.

Chu Hsi 朱熹. Hui-an Hsien-sheng Chu-wen kung wen-chi 晦菴先生朱文
　　　公文集.

Ch'ü T'ung-ssu. 1957. "Chinese Class Structure and its Ideology."
　　　Chinese Thought and Institutions (Chicago), pp. 235-250.

Creel, H.G. 1937. Studies in Early Chinese Culture (Baltimore).

d'Argence, René Yvon Lefebvre. "Ecological Atlas of Southern Sung-Hang-
　　　chou." (Unpublished manuscript).

des Rotours, Robert (trans.). 1962. Histoire de Ngan Lou-chan (Paris).
　　　————— (trans.). 1947. Traité des Fonctionnaires et Traité de
　　　l'Armée, traduits de la nouvelle histoire des T'ang. (2v., Leiden).

Dodds, E.R. 1951. The Greeks and the Irrational (Berkeley).

Dubs, Homer H. (trans.). 1938-1956. The History of the Former Han, a
　　　critical translation with annotations (3v., Baltimore).

Homans, George C. 1964. "Bringing Men Back In." American Sociological
　　　Review 29: pp. 809-818.

Hsü Nai-ch'ang 徐乃昌. 1923. Sung Yüan k'o-chü san-lu 宋元科舉
　　　三錄.

Hu Shih. 1929. "The Establishment of Confucianism as a State Religion
　　　during the Han Dynasty." Journal of the North China Branch of the
　　　Royal Asiatic Society 60: pp. 20-41.

Jeffcott, Colin. 1970. "Sung Hang-chou: Its Growth and Its Governmental
　　　Institutions." (Ph.D. dissertation, Australian National University).

Kracke, Edward A., Jr. 1953. Civil Service in Early Sung China, 960-
　　　1067 (Cambridge).

_____. 1947. "Family vs. Merit in Chinese Civil Service Examinations Under the Empire." Harvard Journal of Asiatic Studies 10: pp. 103-123.

_____. 1957. Translation of Sung Civil Service Titles (Paris).

Kramers, R.P. 1955. "Conservatism and the Transmission of the Confucian Canon." Journal of Oriental Studies 2: pp. 119-132.

Latham, Ronald (trans.). 1958. The Travels of Marco Polo (Baltimore).

Legge, James (trans.). 1865-1872. The Chinese Classics (5v., London).

Levy, Howard S. (trans.). 1961. Biography of Huang Ch'ao (Berkeley).

Li Chieh 李誡. 1925. Ying-tsao fa-shih 營造法式.

Li Hsin-ch'üan 李心傳. 1899. Chien-yen i-lai ch'ao-yeh tsa-chi 建炎以來朝野雜記. In Wu-ying tien chü-chen pan ch'üan-shu 武英殿聚珍版全書.

_____. 1956. Chien-yen i-lai hsi-nien yao-lu 建炎以來繫年要錄 (Shanghai).

Li Tao 李燾. 1881. Hsü-tzu-chih t'ung-chien ch'ang-pien 續資治通鑑長編.

Li Yu 李攸. 1899. Sung-ch'ao shih-shih 宋朝史實. In Wu-ying-tien chü-chen pan ch'üan-shu 武英殿聚珍版全書.

Liebenthal, Walter. 1947. "Wang Pi's New Interpretation of the I CHING." Harvard Journal of Asiatic Studies 10: pp. 124-161.

Liu Cheng 留正. 1968. Huang Sung Chung-hsing liang-ch'ao sheng-cheng 皇宋中興兩朝聖政.

Liu, James T.C. 1967. Ou-Yang Hsiu, An Eleventh-Century NeoConfucianist (Stanford).

Ma Tuan lin 馬端臨. 1859. Wen-hsien t'ung-k'ao 文獻通考.

McKnight, Brian E. 1971. Village and Bureaucracy in Southern Sung China (Chicago).

Moule, A.C. 1957. Quinsai, with Other Notes on Marco Polo (Cambridge).

Nan Sung kuan-ko hsü-lu 南宋館閣續錄. 1886. In Wu-lin ch'ang-ku
    ts'ung-pien 武林掌故叢編.

Pan Ku 班固. Han shu 漢書.

Pulleyblank, Edwin G. 1964. "The Historiographical Tradition." The Legacy
    of China (Oxford), pp. 143-164.

Reischauer, Edwin O. and John K. Fairbank. 1960. A History of East Asia
    (2v., Boston).

Shih O 施鍔. 1886. Ch'un-yu Lin-an chih 淳祐臨安志. In Wu-lin
    ch'ang-ku ts'ung-pien 武林掌故叢編.

Sickman, Laurence and Alexander Soper. 1956. The Art and Architecture of
    China (Baltimore).

Siren, Osvald. 1929. "Chinese Architecture." Encyclopedia Britannica
    14th ed., 5: pp. 556-565.

Sun Feng-chi 孫逢吉. 1934. Chih-kuan fen-chi 職官分紀. In Ssu-k'u
    ch'üan-shu chen-pen 四庫全書珍本.

Sung hui-yao chi-kao 宋會要輯稿. 1967. (Taipei).

Tjan Tjoe-som (trans.). 1949-1952. Po Hu T'ung: The Comprehensive Dis-
    courses in the White Tiger Hall (2v., Leiden).

T'o T'o 脱脱 and others. Sung shih 宋史.

Tsien Tsuen-hsuin. 1952. "A History of Bibliographic Classification in
    China." Library Quarterly 22: pp. 307-324.

_____. 1962. Written on Bamboo and Silk (Chicago).

Wang Kuo-wei 王國維. 1936. Wu-tai liang-sung chien-pen k'ao 五代兩宋監
    本考. In Hai-ning wang-ching-an hsien-sheng i-shu 海寧王靜安
    先生遺書 (Shanghai).

Wang P'u 王溥. 1899. T'ang hui-yao 唐會要. In Wu-ying tien chü-chen
    pen ch'üan-shu 武英殿聚珍版全書.

Wang Yao-ch'en 王堯臣 . 1799. Ch'ung-wen ts'ung-mu 崇文總目 . In Han-yü chai ts'ung-shu

Wang Ying-lin 王應麟 . 1883. Yü hai 玉海

Watson, Burton (trans.). 1961. Records of the Grand Historian of China (2v., New York).

Wu Ch'eng-lo 吳承洛 . 1939. Chung-kuo tu-liang heng-shih 中國度量衡史 (Shanghai).

Wu Kwang-tsing. 1937. "Libraries and Book Collecting in China before the Invention of Printing." T'ien Hsia Monthly 5: pp. 237-260.

_____. 1944. "Scholarship, Book Production and Libraries in China, 618-1644." (Ph.D. dissertation, University of Chicago).

Wu Tzu-mu 吳自牧 . 1886. Meng-liang lu 夢梁錄 . In Wu-lin ch'ang-ku ts'ung-pien 武林掌故叢編 .

Yang Li-ch'ang 楊立誠 and Chin Pu-ying 金步瀛 . 1929. Chung-kuo ts'ung-shu chia-k'ao lüeh 中國叢書家考畧 .

Yang, Lien-sheng. 1952. Money and Credit in China, a Short History (Cambridge).

Yeh Ch'ang-ch'ih 葉昌熾 . 1875-1908. Ts'ang-shu chi-shih shih 藏書紀事詩 . In Ling-chien ko ts'ung-shu 靈鶼閣叢書 .

Yeh Meng-te 葉夢得 . 1573-1620. Shih-lin yen-yü 石林燕語 . In Pai-hai 碑海 .

Yeh Te-hui 葉德輝 . 1920. Shu-lin ch'ing-hua 書林清話 .

Yu Mou 尤袤 . 1849. Sui-ch'u T'ang-shu-mu 遂初堂書目 . In Hai-shan hsien-kuan ts'ung-shu 海山仙館叢書 .

Yü Ying-shih. 1967. Trade and Expansion in Han China (Berkeley).

INDEX

Academician (Hsüeh-shih), 10
Academician-in-waiting (Tai-chih), 10
Academician-in-waiting of the T'ien Chang Pavilion (T'ien-chang ko tai-chih), 10
Academician of the Lung T'u Pavilion (Lung-t'u ko hsüeh-shih), 10
Agency libraries 9, 11
Apprentice (T'ou-ming-jen), 25
Assistant staff author (Chu-tso tso-lang), 18, 26, 27
Assistant writer (Shu-chih kuan), 25
Assistant writer in the Four Collections (Ssu-k'u shu-chih kuan), 25
Associate Reign History editor (T'ung-hsiu kuo-shih), 17
Attendant (K'u-tzu), 37
Auxiliary-academician (Chih-hsüeh-shih), 10
Auxiliary official of the Chao Wen Institute (Chih chao-wen kuan), 19

Bibliography, 8, 16
Biographies (lieh-chuan), 27
Book of Changes (I ching), 6
Book of Filial Piety (Hsiao ching), 25
Book of History (Shu ching), 6, 7
Book of Poetry (Shih ching), 6, 24
Book of Rites (Chou i), 25
Book of Rites (Li chi), 6
Bureau of Bells and Drums (Chung-ku yüan), 19
Bursary office (Kung-shih-k'u), 37

Calendar desk (T'ai-shih an), 19
Canon of orthodox belief, 6–7
Censorship, 8
Ceremonies desk (Chu-pan an), 19
Chao Wen Institute (Chao Wen Kuan), 15, 19
Chi Hsien Library (Chi Hsien Tien), 15, 19
Chief of copyists (Shou-tang kuan), 25
Chüan (roll), 9
Ch'ung Wen Library (Ch'ung Wen Yüan), 15, 19
Clepsydra Office (Ts'e-yen han-i k'o-lou so), 19
Collator of the Imperial Library (Pi-shu sheng chiao-shu lang), 17, 26
Compilation and history area, 17–18
Compiler (Pien-hsiu kuan), 17
Copyist (Cheng-hsi-ming), 25
Copyist Office (Pu-hsieh so), 33
Correcting editor of the Imperial Library (Pi-shu cheng-tzu), 17, 26
Corrector (Shou-ch'üeh hsi-ming), 25

Daily record (jih-li), 10, 19, 20, 26, 27
Daily Record Office (Jih-li so), 10, 18, 19, 27

Desk (an), 19
Diary of activity and repose (ch'i-chü chu), 18
Directive personnel, 20–21, 23, 28, 33, 41, 44
Director of attendants (Chien-k'u-tzu), 37
Director of operative personnel (Tu-k'ung-mu kuan), 25
Director of the Imperial Library (Pi-shu chien), 17, 26
Directorate of Education (Kuo-tzu chien), 7, 15, 32

Examination laureates (Chuang-yüan), 23, 43
Examinations, 20, 22–23, 24, 25, 43
Executive-assistant of the Imperial Library (Pi-shu ch'eng), 15, 17, 26

General services desk (Chih-tsa an), 19

Hang-chou, 12–15
Historical Records (Shih chi), 7, 27
Historiography, 7, 17, 18, 26
History of the Former Han Dynasty (Han shu), 8

Imperial annals (ti-chi), 27
Imperial Archives (Pi-ko), 15, 17, 19, 32, 34, 38
Imperial Library (Pi-shu sheng), 5, 7, 9, 10, 12, 14, 15
Imperial Library area, 15–17
Imperial repositories, 9, 10
Imperial writings, 7, 27, 29
Institute of History (Shih Kuan), 15, 19
Intendant of the Imperial Library (T'i-chü Pi-shu sheng), 17
Intendant of the Reign History Bureau (T'i-chü Kuo-shih yüan), 17

Kung-Sun Hung, 8

Lao-tzu, 24
Librarian of the Imperial Library (Pi-shu lang), 17, 26
Library acquisitions, 8, 10, 11, 27–32, 32–33
Library administration, 8, 18–19
Library attendant (Shu-k'u kuan), 25
Library buildings, 12, 15, 40–41
Library catalogs, 8, 16, 17, 18, 22, 35, 38, 39
Library circulation, 37–39
Library collections, 8, 10, 11, 16, 18, 19, 27, 28, 32, 33, 33–37
Library collections desk (Ching-chi an), 19
Library losses, 8, 9, 10, 11–12
Library personnel, 15, 17, 18, 23–24, 27, 33, 44, 45

Library use, 7–8, 37–39
Liu Hsiang, 8
Liu Hsin, 8

Meng-tzu, 24
monographs (chih), 27

Office of the Calendar (T'ai-shih chü), 19
Operative personnel, 20, 21, 24–26, 27, 33, 42
Orthodox belief, 6–7

Palace courier (Piao-tsou kuan), 25
Palace grounds (ta-nei), 9, 11, 12, 13
Palace libraries, 9
Printing, 5, 7, 18, 28, 32, 34, 35, 37
Private libraries, 37

Records of current government (shih-cheng chi), 18
Reign chronicle (shih-lu), 7, 27, 28–29
Reign Chronicle Bureau (Shih-lu yüan), 10, 27
Reign history (kuo-shih), 7, 27, 29
Reign History Bureau (Kuo-shih yüan), 10, 12, 15, 17, 27, 40
Reign History editor (Hsiu kuo-shih), 17
Rest and contemplation area, 18

Scholarly agencies, 5, 7, 9, 10, 19
Scholarship, 5–6, 6–7, 9, 10, 26–27
Selected documents (hui-yao), 7, 11, 19, 27, 29
Selected Documents Office (Hui-yao so), 10, 18, 19, 27, 35
Senior copyist (Cheng-ming k'ai-shu), 25
Senior corrector (Shou-ch'üeh), 25
Separate Records (Pieh lu), 8
Service area, 18
Service personnel, 20, 21, 26, 42
Shih-ch'ü Pavilion (Shih Ch'ü Ko), 6
Sou-fang depository (sou-fang k'u), 35
Spring and Autumn Annals (Ch'un-ch'iu), 6, 7, 27
Staff author (Chu-tso lang), 26, 27
Standard histories (cheng-shih), 7
Steppe people, 9, 11, 12, 27

Vice-director of Operative Personnel (K'ung-mu kuan), 25
Vice-director of the Imperial Library (Pi-shu shao-chien), 26, 29

Wages, 21, 26
Wen-te Hall (Wen Te Tien) 19
West Hall (Hsi Kuan), 15

Yeh Meng-te, 28, 34

TRANSACTIONS

OF THE

AMERICAN PHILOSOPHICAL SOCIETY

HELD AT PHILADELPHIA
FOR PROMOTING USEFUL KNOWLEDGE

NEW SERIES—VOLUME 64
1974

THE AMERICAN PHILOSOPHICAL SOCIETY
INDEPENDENCE SQUARE
PHILADELPHIA

1974

CONTENTS OF VOLUME 64

PART 1. The "Real Expedición Marítima de la Vacuna" in New Spain and Guatemala. MICHAEL M. SMITH.

PART 2. Bellièvre, Sully, and the Assembly of Notables of 1496. J. RUSSELL MAJOR.

PART 3. The Sacred Officials of the Eleusinian Mysteries. KEVIN CLINTON.

PART 4. Mappae Clavicula: A Little Key to the World of Medieval Techniques. CYRIL STANLEY SMITH and JOHN G. HAWTHORNE.

PART 5. Benjamin Rush: Philosopher of the Revolution. DONALD J. D'ELIA.

PART 6. Ritual Structure and Language Structure of the Todas. MURRAY B. EMENEAU.

PART 7. Gears from the Greeks: The Antikythera Mechanism—A Calendar Computer from ca. 80 B.C. DEREK DE SOLLA PRICE.

PART 8. The Imperial Library in Southern Sung China, 1127–1279: A Study of the Organization and Operation of the Scholarly Agencies in the Central Government. JOHN H. WINKELMAN.